MW00986062

DISCARD

ARMY 101

ARMY 101

Inside ROTC in a Time of War DAVID AXE

The University of South Carolina Press

Published by the University of South Carolina Press
Columbia, South Carolina 29208

www.sc.edu/uscpress

Manufactured in the United States of America

16 15 14 13 12 11 10 09 08 07   10 9 8 7 6 5 4 3 2 1

Library of Congress Cataloging-in-Publication Data

Axe, David.
  Army 101 : inside ROTC in a time of war / David Axe.
      p. cm.
  ISBN-13: 978-1-57003-660-6 (cloth : alk. paper)
  ISBN-10: 1-57003-660-8 (cloth : alk. paper)
  1. University of South Carolina. Army ROTC–History–21st century. I. Title.
  U429.U557A84 2006
  355.2'232071175771–dc22
                                    2006022265

Army 101 is based on the experiences of Army ROTC cadets at the University of South Carolina between 2001 and 2004. Some names have been changed, and some characters are composites. All errors and opinions are the author's alone.

Dedicated to the Gamecock Battalion. Good luck and try not to die.

Contents

Illustrations

ONE

Bang, Bang, You're Dead

It has rained recently and the ground is wet and cold. Lying on his stomach, in the brush alongside a dirt trail, twenty-year-old Jonathan Coe is uncomfortable. But what else is new?

First comes the sensation of cold, piercing the coarse fabric of his fatigues and the soft cotton of his brown T-shirt. Then the moisture, puckering his skin as it crawls the length of his body. Sweat mixes with cold rainwater to produce a salty soup that's neither hot nor cold but somehow worse than either. It collects in the butt crack, the armpits, the insides of his leather boots. The crotch.

Amazingly, he barely notices. Between the heavy loads, the rough terrain, the insects, the hot sun, the bad chow, and sleeping on the ground in the rain, he's been uncomfortable for days. After a while the misery fades to a sort of background buzz.

Besides, a little cold, a little sweat, a cramp or two—these are the least of his problems. Somewhere up the road is an enemy patrol, and reports say they are headed this way.

Two days ago he saw them. They were a ragged bunch, dressed in faded green uniforms similar to his but sloppier. Young and confused mostly. But they were well led and well armed. Armed, in fact, much like Coe and his platoon, with M16s and machine guns.

Stars and a sliver of moon are the only sources of light. Fog from the evaporating rain obscures the path, save for a short stretch just a few yards from where Coe and his young soldiers lie concealed in twigs and dead leaves.

They have a name for that little naked length of path: "kill zone." It's one of those chillingly matter-of-fact Army terms.

There are about twenty soldiers hunkered in the woods on one side of the path. Coe's eight soldiers are hunkered in the underbrush around him. All of them are restless, sometimes fidgeting with their rifles or nodding off and then jerking awake a few seconds later. Despite how much Coe's platoon leader stressed noise- and light-discipline during his briefing, several soldiers flip the switches on their M16s from single-shot to safety and back. Others light up their watches to check the time. Ghostly green watch faces hover in the darkness. Coe wants to hiss at his squad to shut up and lie still, but every distant snapping twig convinces him that the enemy is about to enter the kill zone, and if someone's going to fuck up and betray the platoon's position, it's not going to be him. Let somebody else get them all shot. Like the platoon leader. A terrified young man no older than Coe and no more experienced. He's crouching nearby with his wide eyes darting left and right like in some kind of cartoon. His eyes come to rest on Coe, and then on every member of Coe's squad. He then checks the other squad in the center and the two teams on the wings, whose job it is to provide security against infiltration and to pick off fleeing survivors after the machine gun has done its work.

The machine gun. An M60 to be exact. A Vietnam War–era relic that weighs thirty pounds and bruises the knees of the unfortunates picked to haul it. Soldiers call it the "pig." With its two-man crew, the pig is the platoon leader's most important tool, what the Army blithely calls "the most-casualty-producing weapon." According to the textbook, a handy little guide to killing known as Field Manual 7-8, the leader should initiate the ambush with said most-casualty-producing weapon. The explosion of sound and light from an M60 is the other soldiers' cue to open fire with their M16s. The idea is to saturate the kill zone in solid sheets of hot metal for just a few lethal seconds. And then. . . .

And then it gets interesting. One squad, the near-side team, rushes through the kill zone. Next comes Coe's squad, the far-side team. They hop over the near-siders and take up positions on the opposite side of the path, where they await the platoon leader's instructions. What ensues is supposed to be a lightning-fast dance of small teams tasked with searching and stripping enemy dead and taking prisoner any wounded. These the Army calls "actions on the objective," that is, further fucking up the poor bastards you just got done shooting.

That's the Army for you: a linguistic mishmash of brutal simplicity and convoluted legalese.

In theory, actions on the objective take only seconds. In reality, it's a bit longer. People trip. People run into each other. People get confused. Corpses, wounded enemies, and prisoners refuse to cooperate. Any number of things can go wrong. And considering the inexperience of Coe's soldiers, they most certainly *will* go wrong.

Sometimes Coe can't believe where he is and what he's doing. He's still a college student, for God's sake, a chemistry major from Darlington, South Carolina, a tiny town most famous for its NASCAR racetrack and illegal dog-fighting rings. He shares a dorm room with his twin brother. He's dating his high school sweetheart. How in the world did he end up face down in the weeds with an M16, waiting to shoot at a bunch of people who are probably just as bewildered as he is?

Twigs snap. Soldiers twitch. Someone flips their safety switch. After so many hours of filtering random noises all around him, Coe can't tell any more what's important and what's just Mother Nature's pranks or some eighteen-year-old jerk-off with a full bladder on the right wing.

Then he sees them.

They move like specters. The soft sounds of their feet on the path seem out of sync with the blurry motion of their legs. Their faces are shadowy masks. Their uniforms glow weakly in the moonlight. Here and there, metal glints.

Coe goes tense, as does everyone around him. Glancing at his platoon leader, Coe sees the young man's hand hover over the shoulder of the M60 gunner lying beside him. All he has to do is drop his hand and the pig will roar, Coe will squeeze the trigger of his M16, his soldiers will follow suit, and the tense stillness of the woods will turn into instant pandemonium.

Coe can't wait. He's had enough of this shit. But even as every instinct screams "Go! Go! Go!" Coe *does* wait, silently but impatiently, and so does the platoon leader. They wait because they both hear voices in their heads—the same voice in fact. It's the combined voice of their instructors, seasoned sergeants and officers all, telling them to wait until the entire string of specters has emerged from the fog and stepped into the kill zone.

Which happens just seconds later.

The platoon leader drops his hand, and the whole world explodes in blinding yellow light and sounds so loud that everything else goes mute: M16s popping off all around him, soldiers bellowing, enemy soldiers crying out as they fall to the ground flailing. It's a bizarre pantomime.

Amid the chaos, Coe realizes he's already expended a full magazine. Almost without thinking he reaches into his ammo pouch, fumbles until his hand touches metal, slaps in the fresh magazine, and keeps shooting.

After that everything just seems to *happen*. The platoon leader signals the M60 gunner to cease firing. He stands and orders the soldiers on the wings to watch for stragglers and escapees. Then he yells, "Near side!"

Nine soldiers clamber to their feet and hustle across the path, firing on the run. When the near-side team has gained the opposite side and thrown themselves to the ground, the platoon leader makes eye contact with Coe and calls out, "Far side!"

Coe scrambles to his feet, slipping in the wet underbrush. His soldiers see him stand and automatically stand, too. That's how it works. If your squad leader moves, you move. If he shoots, you shoot. If he runs headlong into a kill zone heaped with dead and wounded enemy soldiers, you do, too.

He feels his feet pound the earth. He hears his heartbeat in his ears. He sees the shapes of fallen enemy soldiers on the moonlit path only yards away. And he sees one of them moving, rolling back and forth, moaning.

The man's in pain. Coe's instinct is to stop, to help, to comfort a fellow human being. But tonight there's something more powerful than instinct at work. It's called training.

Looming over the wounded enemy soldier, looking down at his wide eyes and boyish features, Coe does exactly what he's been trained to do. He aims his M16. He tightens his finger on the trigger. Then he points his rifle away from his enemy, relaxes his finger and says, "Bang, bang."

Coe has been instructed not to fire his blanks near another person. Gas and tiny particles from the empty training rounds can inflict burns at close range.

That and they're fucking *loud*.

"Bang," Coe says. "You're dead."

His "enemy" grimaces, rolls his eyes back in his head and goes still. But he's still breathing and—judging from the staccato rise and fall of his chest—even laughing. If not for the ringing in his ears, Coe could hear him. It isn't the first time this pretend enemy combatant has died in the past couple days. And it won't be the last.

It's the second day of a three-day field training exercise, or FTX, in the pine and oak forests of sprawling Fort Jackson near Columbia, the bustling capital of South Carolina. Fort Jackson's fifty thousand acres are treasured by state conservationists as a haven for wood ducks, several varieties of foxes, and a species of fish called a chubsucker. But in these woods, on this cold night in March 2003, an even stranger and rarer breed is on the prowl: the pride of the University of South Carolina's Gamecock Battalion. Cadets of the U.S. Army's Reserve Officers' Training Corps. Undergrads with machine guns.

Coe's a junior, what the Army calls a Military Science III cadet, or MSIII, and as a competent cadet with a good head on his shoulders, he's the exception to the rule. Most of his squadmates are freshmen and sophomores, MSIs and 'IIs. By and large they're clueless. The enemy soldiers are MSIs and 'IIs led by a couple of MSIVs, seniors, and the only reasons they appear more confident than the others are (1) good leadership by experienced seniors, and (2) as the Opposing Force, or OPFOR, they're encouraged to swagger, improvise, and generally act like Jean-Claude Van Damme in his B-movie heyday.

Everyone's equipment is authentic: real M16s, real M60s, real uniforms and helmets and combat boots. The only thing that's not real is the ammunition. Instead of packing a metal slug at its tip, each round is pinched at the top and hollow. So instead of propelling lethal rounds out of their barrels, the cadets' weapons just go "pop." It's the same kind of technology Hollywood uses in action movies.

Come to think of it, everything about this FTX is like an action movie: clumsy blocking, bad dialogue, long stretches of nothing but boring exposition, between which are sandwiched hackneyed action sequences where anonymous characters fire wildly and die unconvincingly. The bad blocking is a result of eighty half-trained college students trying to look like they know what they're doing when in fact they don't. The cheesy dialogue is the fault of Hollywood itself, which has made clichés of all the Army's traditional commands and terminology. Among the pines echo orders:

"Incoming!"

"Take cover!"

"Alpha Team, bound forward!"

"Cease fire!"

"Ammo! I need ammo!"

Meanwhile cadets trip over branches, fall into holes, drop their rifles and rucksacks, get tangled in briars, and trudge around in the dark in their ill-fitting uniforms and helmets looking grumpy and confused. It's enough to make a seasoned soldier squirm. And there are plenty of seasoned soldiers around to squirm. Not even Cadet Command, the understaffed Army organization in charge of all ROTC cadets—30,000 at 270 colleges and universities as of 2003 —would send poorly trained college kids to run around the woods at night unsupervised. In addition to twenty or so MSIVs, there are eight or nine officers and noncommissioned officers with a combined seventy-five years of Army service. These are the cadre—role models, instructors, and parental figures for a diverse group of 80 cadets. The officer cadre themselves are products of ROTC. Only ten or twenty years earlier, *they* were the ones running around the woods with rifles yelling, "Bang, bang!" at pretend enemies.

So they understand. But it doesn't make the cadets' antics any less distressing. After all, theirs is an Army at war, and in only months or years, these amateurs will take their places on the front lines in the Philippines, Afghanistan, and wherever else the U.S. Army finds itself committed in the ever-expanding "War on Terror." This very month has seen a coalition of armed forces invade Iraq. Among the deployed are around 250,000 American soldiers, including more than 10,000 ROTC grads.

Four years may seem like a long time to turn civilians into soldiers. But when these civilians are college students with classes, jobs, and social lives— all of which the Army considers vital to its cadets' educations—then four years isn't long at all. There's a lot of ground to cover. Coe may be pretty close to competent, but many of his peers sure aren't. And as Coe clears the kill zone on this foggy, nighttime ambush exercise, with giggling casualties behind him and his terrified teammates looking up at him from all around, one thing is clear: ROTC has its work cut out for it.

Citizen-Soldiers 2

There are one hundred thousand officers in the U.S. Army. Every year seven thousand leave the service, and seven thousand others take their places.

Most people think officers all come from the United States Military Academy, better known as West Point, the official college of the U.S. Army. In fact West Point fulfills only a fraction of the Army's needs, commissioning around a thousand officers per year. Another couple thousand come from Officer Candidates School, a fourteen-week course that awards commissions to enlisted soldiers. But most prospective officers in the Army—and in the Navy, Marine Corps, and Air Force, for that matter—attend civilian colleges and universities and receive their military training through ROTC, essentially minoring in the military while pursuing a regular academic major and earning their commissions along with their degrees. With facilities and all but a handful of instructors provided by host schools, ROTC is a real bargain, producing a commissioned officer in four years at a fraction of the cost of West Point with its famous $250,000 educations.

But there are other advantages. The U.S. military has been an all-volunteer professional force since 1973. And even when the draft was still in effect— during the Civil War, the World Wars, Korea, and Vietnam—significant numbers of enlistees were volunteers. The volunteer spirit has long characterized the American military, which has always prided itself in its "citizen-soldiers."

It's an idea with roots in the American Revolution, when farmers and craftsmen put down their tools and picked up muskets and marched to war with their neighbors. To this day the chiefs of the armed forces are all civilians, and so is the commander in chief, the president. Founded on principles opposed to tyranny of all kinds, the United States is careful to subject its soldiers to its civilians and, at the same time, to keep the two classes closely entwined. In theory, American soldiers are just American civilians in different clothes. Their values are the same: life, liberty, and the pursuit of happiness. You can trust

American soldiers to act in the best interests of average citizens because they are themselves average citizens.

This is why ROTC is so important. ROTC cadets are students first and soldiers second. They're average kids in uniform. And while that may mean somewhat slipshod military training, at least in a tactical sense, the U.S. military has always prized flexible minds and strong moral character over killing skills. It's telling that the Army's core values—loyalty, duty, respect, service, honor, integrity, and courage—do not include *lethality*.

Thus, ROTC is the best system for preparing officers for military service. Like any degree program, it emphasizes academics, time management, flexibility, and balance. Where West Point cadets live, breathe and dream Army Army Army, ROTC cadets move in and out of the military mode. One day they're in uniform running around with rifles. The next they're in their jeans and T-shirts trying to stay awake in English 101. That night they're at a party drinking too much, hitting on members of the opposite sex (or, in very rare cases, the same sex), and learning the hard way what it means to be a civil person in a civil society.

While it's true that cadets are students before they're soldiers, it's not unfair to call ROTC the hardest minor ever. This is, after all, the U.S. Army, so a little rigor is in order. Cadets wake around 5:30 A.M. several days a week for physical training, or PT. They participate in weekly labs in which they organize into small groups and practice basic military skills, like marching and fighting in squads and platoons. Sometimes they train on weekends, wandering around the woods with maps or rappelling from towers. And they spend at least one summer at Army schools. Meanwhile, they take classes on military history and theory for regular academic credit. And they live under codes of conduct both formal and informal. On one hand they're accountable to their cadre, the officers and NCOs of their resident department of military science, the academic department that at most universities gives cadre adjunct instructor status. On the other hand cadets answer to their peers, whose standards and expectations are, if not higher than the department's, at least different—and no less real.

From the standpoint of the average college student, whose four (or three or five or six) years as an undergraduate are perhaps the least regimented and often the sheer sloppiest of their lives, ROTC may seem a little strange. One day the guy down the hall looks and acts just like you do. Sure, his hair is a little shorter and he seems to go to bed earlier than everyone else, but for the most part he's just an average joe.

Then one day he comes strutting out of his dorm room in pressed fatigues, spit-shined boots, and a snazzy black beret. He holds his head high. He swings his arms with strange precision. He says he's headed to lab, which in your experience means slouching over a Bunsen burner for a couple of hours. Later you pass him on the grassy square in the middle of campus. He's standing ramrod-straight in front of several orderly rows of identically dressed students. And he's barking like a dog in a language only vaguely English, giving orders that the rows respond to in perfect unison. He says, "Left, face!" and everyone turns on their heels like cogs in a human machine.

He turns, too. He snaps his head to face the columns.

"Forward, march!"

Just like that, the whole formation steps out, perfectly synchronized. And the leader, that guy from down the hall, starts to sing. That's right, *sing*. His song goes something like this:

R-O-T-C
Patch on my shoulder
Pick up your books and follow me
I am the wanna-be infantry

Like so many modern institutions, the Reserve Officers' Training Corps was born on the battlefields of World War I. The year 1916 saw 620,000 British and French soldiers fall dead or wounded advancing barely ten miles at the Battle of the Somme, during which 500,000 German soldiers also became casualties. Another 180,000 Commonwealth and French soldiers were killed or wounded in a doomed attempt to seize the Dardanelles. Meanwhile, restricted submarine warfare resulted in only a few dozen German U-boats sinking a thousand ships by 1916, including the ocean liners *Lusitania* and *Sussex*, and causing real fear for the first time in Britain's passive cousin across the sea. Before the U-boat assault, most Americans were content to let the Europeans work out their own problems. But submarine warfare, with its unseen assailants threatening civilians and sailors alike, terrified the maritime United States. For a hundred years it had been protected by the oceans. For the first time, that protection seemed impotent.

With each passing month, America's neutrality looked increasingly unrealistic. The time would come for intervention. And when it did, America must be ready.

But in 1916 America was definitely *not* ready. Its army numbered only 140,000, barely 5 percent of Great Britain's total. Its navy had only 245 antiquated ships versus Britain's modern fleet of more than 400. And in a day when fighter aces like Albert Ball and the Baron von Richthofen dominated the skies, shooting down dozens of enemy aircraft and balloons, America had no air corps to speak of.

All that would begin to change with the passage of the National Defense Act of 1916. Among its many provisions, it collapsed the heretofore separate Army, Army Reserve, and National Guard into one U.S. Army with multiple branches.

In a year, the Army's numbers swelled to four million. This massively expanded Army required around a quarter-million officers. To supply this new officer class, the Army created ROTC, which itself relied on an old model of military education dating back a hundred years to 1819, when Norwich University was founded as the United States' first private military college.

The military model of education, which stressed discipline, physical fitness, and hierarchical social structures, was popular in the nineteenth century. Soon Virginia Military Institute, the Citadel, and the University of Tennessee joined Norwich as military colleges. And the Land Grant Act of 1862 required all schools founded as a result of the act to offer military instruction. In the 1880s and '90s the University of Missouri pioneered the summer camp model of training and even had a separate corps for female trainees. By 1900 more than one hundred universities in the United States offered or required military training. While standards varied greatly, and results even more so, and while there was no formal relationship between these military colleges and the Army, by 1916 there was a basic structure in place on which to build an official, rigorous, university-based officer-training program.

ROTC expanded quickly. By the beginning of 1917 there were units in operation on forty-six campuses overseeing 40,000 cadets. Both numbers increased rapidly. In 1917 and '18, ROTC units fed around 100,000 officers into the Army. And among the 260,000 dead and wounded Americans in World War I were thousands of officers.

Cataclysmic casualty rates aside, ROTC was a success. In the interwar period it continued on a smaller scale. And at the outbreak of World War II in 1941, 56,000 ROTC officers were called to active duty. By 1945 that number had doubled, accounting for 12 percent of all Army officers.

In its first fifty years, ROTC's units were tailored to provide officers to specific branches. So Furman University in Greenville, South Carolina, had an armor ROTC unit. Georgia Tech had units for infantry, coastal artillery and the signal, motor transport, and air corps. After World War II, Gen. Dwight Eisenhower, then chief of the War Department, signed an order transferring seventy-eight air corps ROTC units to the new U.S. Air Force. In 1964 Congress passed the ROTC Revitalization Act, which funded the first scholarships.

The Vietnam War nearly doomed ROTC. Enrollment plummeted 75 percent between 1967 and 1972. Many campuses saw massive protests against resident units. Desperately scrambling to preserve the corps, in 1973 the Army completely overhauled the training and structure of ROTC, increasing scholarships, offering cadets slots in specialized schools like Airborne, and admitting women for the first time.

Recovery was rapid. The total number of ROTC units increased from 297 to 416 between 1978 and 1983, in which year around eighty thousand cadets were enrolled. And in 1986 Cadet Command was created to oversee Army ROTC programs nationwide. All told, between 1945 and 2000, around four hundred thousand students participated in ROTC.

The Gamecock Battalion—named after the University of South Carolina's mascot, a fighting rooster—has a history as long and complicated as any ROTC unit. Though formally established in 1917, the Gamecock Battalion inherited a long tradition of military training that is nearly as old as the university itself.

South Carolina College, the predecessor of the University of South Carolina (USC), was founded in 1801 by the General Assembly of the state in order to educate future entrepreneurs, scientists, scholars, and politicians—as well as to unite disparate subcultures scattered throughout the state. It was no accident that the college was to be located in the shadow of the statehouse, the seat of the S.C. government. If South Carolina's central government was to mean anything, reasoned the General Assembly, it must play a role in educating leaders of the state's diverse communities.

For fifty years, the college grew in fits and starts. And while it was not a formal military college like the Citadel and, later, Clemson, it *did* have a resident cadet company, a voluntary paramilitary club of sorts for inculcating a military ethos in potential officers. However, in 1856 the cadet company played a role in a student riot that prompted widespread reforms at the college. Among other reforms was the disbanding of the cadet company. And for the next several years there was no military organization at all on campus—formal, informal, or otherwise.

All of that changed in 1860. With secessionist sentiment spreading throughout the state—indeed, throughout the South—the college's trustees granted permission to the student body to organize its own company for one year. In light of the old cadet company's riotous behavior, and reflecting a strain of pacifism among the college's eight full-time faculty, the trustees' permission carried a number of provisos severely limiting the company's authority to drill. State government slyly undermined the college's efforts to restrict its cadets by supplying the cadet company with one hundred muskets, courtesy of the state arsenal.

On the morning of February 11, 1861, the cadet company gathered at 9:00 to celebrate the official formation of the Confederacy. Soon Union-held Fort Sumter in Charleston Harbor was under bombardment by Confederate troops, and South Carolina College's cadets were eager to join the fight. When the faculty refused to grant them permission, the cadets left anyway and approached the governor as a company of volunteers. They were promptly shipped to Sullivan's Island, near Charleston, where they were tasked with defending the beaches against a possible Union assault. Eventually a professor joined them as chaplain. In three months the company saw combat only once, thwarting a half-hearted federal probe of the island. In May the governor ordered the cadets back to the college, just in time for summer vacation.

By now, the action in the "War of Northern Aggression" was in Virginia. The cadet company presented itself to the government again, but this time the governor said he would accept their service only with the faculty's consent. But the faculty refused to exercise any control whatsoever over its students during vacation, so the cadet company disbanded and its members simply joined other units marching for the front.

By now, war had whittled South Carolina College's student body to a skeleton of its former self. Every effort by the faculty to reconstitute the college was undermined by another wave of student enlistments. Meanwhile, the occasional faculty member joined the exodus. Several professors were wounded. A couple died. No one made much effort to keep track of how many students or former students perished. It was hard to define "student" when hardly anyone stayed at the college very long.

The war interfered in other ways. In 1862, Confederate authorities seized campus buildings for the army, turning several into wards for as many as two thousand sick and wounded soldiers. With its students off fighting and dying and its buildings full of casualties, it seemed things couldn't get much worse for South Carolina College.

Then came Sherman.

The war was already going badly for the Confederacy when Union general William Tecumseh Sherman led an army deep into the South, burning and pillaging as he went. In February 1865, he arrived in Columbia and blasted the statehouse with cannons. Perhaps coincidentally, around the time of Sherman's arrival, massive fires swept through Columbia.

Little survived. Fortunately for the many wounded, by this time including Union troops captured by the Confederacy, the college escaped undamaged. Sherman's assault and the subsequent fire had a profound effect nonetheless. Refugees took up residence in vacant dormitories, and many stayed for as long as two years. And any hopes the faculty had of restoring the college were dashed. There was no longer a railroad in town. Communications were devastated. Travel was dangerous if not impossible. In May, Union troops occupied the campus. And when the war finally ended, potential students had far more urgent concerns than education. Occupation and reconstruction brought desperation and poverty to—or rather sustained them in—South Carolina.

It would be decades before South Carolina College returned to health. In the interim, it reorganized along university lines, emphasizing research over the old collegiate boarding-school experience. By 1916 the new University of South Carolina was again thriving.

Just in time for another war.

The faculty, some of whom had fought in the Civil War and all of whom recognized the ruin that the conflict had inflicted on the school, were understandably hostile to another round of militarization. So in 1916, when the S.C. National Guard was mobilized to fight in Mexico and several students were forced to abandon the college in order to serve, the faculty grew defensive. But the student body for the most part felt differently. With the war in Europe only intensifying and ROTC units forming all over the United States to fuel the Army's rapid expansion, the faculty soon caved to overwhelming student sentiment. In 1917 USC formally invited the War Department to organize an ROTC unit on campus.

It didn't last long. In December 1918, with the war over, the Gamecock Battalion disbanded. Twenty-eight students had died in Mexico and Europe since 1917. The university planted trees in their memory and erected several memorials. In the immediate aftermath of the war, a sense of grief seemed to dominate the campus. It only got worse when influenza swept through Columbia, claiming several students. So it was with some reluctance that the student body welcomed ROTC when the Army reestablished the Gamecock Battalion in 1919. Local feelings aside, ROTC had proved a success—an efficient system for rapidly culling officers from America's colleges and universities.

ROTC was here to stay. And when the Japanese attacked Pearl Harbor in 1941, drawing the United States into another global war, ROTC provided a framework for USC's contribution to the effort. Academic calendars were accelerated, new training programs were instituted, and USC settled into four long years of churning out officers for the meat grinder.

In 1944 the first survivors began to return home. The war in Europe ended in May 1945. The Pacific war wrapped in August. Between 1945 and 1947, returning GIs boosted annual enrollment at USC from 1,420 to as many as 5,000. Enrollment never really slackened after that.

USC was growing. And not just in terms of size. The thousands of grizzled war vets making up the majority of the student body wanted nothing to do with ROTC and had little patience for authority of any sort. The Gamecock Battalion kept a low profile for a few years. Meanwhile old soldiers forced concessions on the USC administration, winning relaxed regulation of student conduct and more power for student government. In a small way it was a preview of the 1970s, another turbulent time at USC, and another period when ROTC lay low.

The restlessness of the '70s started at Fort Jackson, where the Army was training thousands of draftees for the fighting in Vietnam. Disgruntled soldiers, alienated by the Army and scared of dying, gathered in dozens of tiny watering holes and coffee shops that cropped up all over Columbia. Here they smoked pot, sipped espresso, and talked politics and revolution with hippies, students, and radical agitators just passing through town. The most notorious coffee shop was a little place called UFO. Fearing an honest-to-God revolution, in early 1970 the city conspired to shut down UFO and arrest its proprietors. Undeterred, the soldiers and radicals started gathering at USC's student union, the Russell House, instead. Thus leftist agitation came to traditionally conservative USC, culminating in a series of drug busts and a march by drug advocates on the university president's house in April.

It was not a good time to be in ROTC. And for much of the decade, cadets kept a low profile. But soon the 1980s arrived and with them a total change in the political mood on campus. ROTC settled into a twenty-year period of stability. Enrollment was steady, standards stayed high, and the lack of any real wars meant public attitudes toward ROTC oscillated between positive and ambivalent.

Then the World Trade Center towers fell, the United States invaded Afghanistan, and the War on Terror spread its own brand of terror. ROTC was caught in the middle as public opinion became polarized. And in March 2003 the American-led coalition invaded Iraq.

That's when things got complicated.

Dreams of Flight 3

Back in the Fort Jackson woods, Jonathan Coe is five minutes from epiphany.

Coe and eight other cadets are crouched in a single-file line behind a bored sergeant at the edge of a fog-shrouded, moonlit field. They are miles from anything. The only sounds are the chirps and trills of strange insects, the rustling of mysterious mammals in the underbrush, and the shifting of nervous bodies. A few miles away lies the city of Columbia, with its raucous nightlife, its half-dozen colleges and universities, and its three interstates. Three hundred thousand people live just outside Fort Jackson's fence. But deep in the woods, late at night, Coe and the others feel like they're the last ten people on earth.

At least they have each other.

ROTC can be boring. It can be exhausting. Like any arm of the federal government, it can be illogical and frustrating. But one thing it never is, for Coe at least, is lonely. For every trial and inconvenience that results from being a part-time soldier and a full-time student, there's always at least one person who understands. And in the Gamecock Battalion, there are as many as a hundred. The Army's slogan may be "An Army of One," but really it's anything but. There are more than a million men and women in the U.S. Army, and they all have at least one thing in common: they're in the Army. As simple and obvious as it sounds, there's tremendous power in belonging to such a large group, especially one with such a long history. There's an emotion many people outside the military don't understand, an emotion that makes men fight and die not for their country or some political cause, but for the guy next to him in the foxhole.

Belonging.

It may be cliché, but it's real, and it's the reason Jonathan Coe can huddle in the woods on a cold night miles from civilization and not feel alone. Crouched around him are eight kids and one grizzled sergeant who know just how he feels.

It's no coincidence that many ROTC cadets are in fraternities. Coe is in one of USC's historically black fraternities, Alpha Phi Alpha, and so are a dozen other cadets. The same need to belong draws kids to the Army *and* to the Greek system. While ROTC's sort of like a fraternity with guns, there are key differences. Where many frat boys waste their days drinking and partying and growing soft around the middle, ROTC cadets wake at dawn, run a dozen miles a week, spend weekends in the woods, and worry about haircuts and uniforms. Sure, there's plenty of drinking and partying in ROTC, especially after FTXs, but it's drinking with a purpose in a fraternity with a purpose—the biggest, meanest frat on the planet: thirty-thousand-strong, armed to the teeth, and built to make officers out of college kids.

Belonging. The idea is enough to make Jonathan Coe's heart pump faster. But since when did his heart sound so loud?

There's a vast slapping sound, a sound like the world's largest grandmother beating the world's largest dirty rug in fast forward. Coe cranes his neck to scan the star-sprinkled sky and spots red and yellow lights twinkling in the distance over the trees. They could be from a tower, or even an airplane, if they weren't moving so fast. In seconds, the lights and the source of the sound are on top of him. A cold wind whips the underbrush and sets the trees swaying. It's a UH-60 Blackhawk helicopter, and it looks bigger and weirder than any Coe has seen in photographs and movies.

Even in the darkness it's clear that the chopper's as long as a school bus and as sleek as a sports car. But there the automotive analogies end, because unlike any car, this thing is *alive*. Its four main rotor blades whip the fog. Its tail rotor is a solid disk reflecting the moonlight. It hovers over the field like a metal dragonfly, then wobbles and rears its pointed head as it flairs and touches down.

Twigs, leaves, dirt, and fog scatter in the windstorm. Watching the dark green helicopter kneel impatiently in the middle of the field, Coe can hardly believe that such an improbable machine not only flies, but flies so fast and moves so nimbly.

Coe realizes he's smiling. He looks around and sees his fellow cadets are smiling, too.

A door on the right side of the chopper slides open and man in a green jumpsuit and a bulbous helmet hops out. It's the crew chief. He's holding something, a cord attached to his helmet. With the cord in one hand he scuttles to a point on the chopper's fuselage and plugs in. Now he's connected to the helicopter by the cord, and apparently talking to the pilots through a microphone near his chin as he bends over and hustles towards Coe and the others. When he spots them he raises a hand and motions.

Come forward.

Led by their sergeant, Coe and the others jog single-file to meet the crew chief mid-field. Over the slap of the rotors and the subtler whine of the chopper's twin engines, it's impossible to hear anything else, so the crew chief just makes faces and gestures.

Crouch.

Board one at a time.

Don't touch ANYTHING.

Like everyone in the Army, Coe has heard stories, like how a Huey's rotors flexed on landing in Vietnam and decapitated a decorated pilot. And how an officer in Iraq pulled the wrong handle trying to get out of a Blackhawk and accidentally popped out all the emergency windows. Coe knows just how fragile and dangerous helicopters can be. He's read about the choppers lost in Iraq in recent weeks:

On March 24 an Apache attack helicopter suffers mechanical problems and crash-lands near Karbala, Iraq, only 70 miles from Baghdad. The crew, Ronald Young and David Williams, are taken prisoner. The same day a swarm of 34 Apaches on a mission over Karbala is ambushed by hundreds of Iraqi troops firing machine guns and rifles into the air. Twenty-seven helicopters are peppered with gunfire and one loses an engine to a rocket-propelled grenade. The attack is called off and the Apaches limp back to their base smoking and trailing debris.

On March 25 two helicopters, an Apache and a Blackhawk, go missing in a sandstorm while supporting coalition troops. There is no word yet on the fates of the crews.

On March 28 two Apaches and two Kiowa reconnaissance helicopters crash-land in a sandstorm after intense fighting around Karbala. One Apache rolls onto its back, throwing huge chunks of twisted metal into a Blackhawk parked nearby, and one crewmember breaks a leg.

Everyone knows helicopters are dangerous. So it's all good advice the crew chief gives, and it's exactly the kind of thing Coe is used to in his third year in the Army. It's been said there's no place safer than in the middle of a live-fire Army exercise, because no organization stresses safety and manages risk quite like the U.S. Army.

Somehow that never quite rang true with Coe.

Regardless, in this case the crew chief's wasting his breath. For hours before there were any real helicopters anywhere nearby, Coe and the rest of the Gamecock Battalion rehearsed loading and unloading, using a square patch of dirt to simulate the cabin of a Blackhawk. The cadets were divided into groups of nine called "chalks." An instructor was tapped to head each chalk. It was his job to communicate with the crew chief, lead the nine cadets to their Black-hawk, and see them safely into their seats.

Now it's happening for real. Outside the chopper's cabin, Coe and the other eight cadets drop their bulky rucksacks at their sergeant's feet before climbing in and taking a seat on one of the little nylon hammocks that pass as seat in the U.S. military. There are nylon straps that come over the shoulder and around the torso, and buckle into a quick-release disk over the midsection. When every-one is seated, the sergeant tosses in the rucksacks then climbs in himself. He makes eye contact with everybody, just to make sure, then flashes the crew chief a thumbs-up.

The crew chief shuts the door.

Strapped into his own special seat now, with his headset plugged into the chopper's interior, the crew chief speaks into his microphone. Coe imagines the seasoned S.C. Army National Guard pilots buckled into the Blackhawk's cockpit, surrounded by lights and gauges and all the high-tech whiz-bangs that make a $20-million helicopter tick. He imagines their relief when the crew chief gives them the okay to return to their natural environment. Coe knows that many Guard pilots have thousands of flying hours under their belts; he can only dream how an entire year in the air changes a man.

Seconds later the whole world falls away outside the Blackhawk's square windows, and Coe finds out what it feels like to fly.

It's like a roller-coaster ride, smooth in places, bumpy in others, noisy, and impossibly fast. And it tickles, especially when those smart-assed National Guard pilots decide to treat their human cargo to a low-level swoop over Fort Jackson's forest. Peering through the windows, Coe sees two shades of black slipping by. The darker of the shades is the ground, that hard boring mass to which Coe has been unfortunately anchored his entire life.

Until now.

The flight lasts only a few minutes, but they're the most amazing minutes of his life. At some point before the Blackhawk reluctantly returns to the earth, Coe realizes he's made up his mind. Leave the ambushes and machine gun massacres to somebody else, like maybe those gung ho snake eaters from Mor-ris and Benedict, two historically-black colleges too small for their own ROTC units that send cadets to train at USC instead. There are three or four cadets in Coe's class that are known and feared for their strange desire to get into ground combat. As far as Coe is concerned, they're welcome to it. He doesn't care if the Army idolizes its infantrymen. He doesn't care if flying is just as dan-gerous but less prestigious than hauling a rucksack and a rifle for a living. He doesn't care that aviators are considered the pretty boys of the military. God and the U.S. Army willing, Jonathan Coe is going to be an aviator.

But first he has to pass midterms.

School's hard enough when it's all you've got to do. But for Coe, school's just part of the equation. As a junior he's got three PT sessions, two hours of classroom instruction, and a two-hour lab every week. Technically speaking, he devotes only seven hours per week to ROTC, not counting FTXs. It's a selling point of ROTC that it's not very time consuming. But like many selling points, it's a lie. Because for every hour you spend at lab or PT there's at least an hour of preparation and recovery. You've got to shine those boots, press those uniforms, and pack that rucksack. You've got to review your notes, prepare your briefings, and go over your drill and ceremony in your head, at least, and maybe even spend a few minutes marching around your dorm issuing orders to yourself just to make sure you've got it all right. Afterwards, you've got to shower for a good long time to get the mud and sweat off your skin and the bugs out of your hair. ROTC is easily the most time consuming of Coe's many activities. It's worse than his classes. It's worse than his frat. It's a bigger chunk out of his day than eating and relaxing and even studying. Despite that, for three years he's managed to keep his grades up. But if he slips up, lets his GPA drop below 3.0 or fails a class, he'll lose his Army scholarship.

Which is exactly what happens a year later, in the spring of 2004. Coe fails a French exam, which, despite his having a B average otherwise, means he fails the course. Red flags go up down at Legare College, the 120-year-old building housing the Department of Military Science. Coe's commanding officer, Lt. Col. John Moring, the chair of the department, calls the embarrassed senior in to his office.

"You know what we've got to do," Moring says.

"I know."

Coe's scholarship is suspended. Fortunately, this is his last semester, and he can afford the tuition—barely. And since by now he's already received his assignment in the Army, all he has to do is graduate. No single failing grade is going to keep that from happening. After four years of struggling to juggle school, ROTC, and an approximation of a social life, Coe's nearly finished, inasmuch as finishing means beginning. It's easy to forget sometimes that ROTC, his degree, and everything he's doing here is just preparation for his Army career. Sure, it's been hard. But it's about to get harder. For in December 2003 Coe gets word from Accessions Command, the inscrutable office of colonels and spreadsheets that assigns cadets' jobs in the Army.

He got it. He got Aviation.

What a relief. Now all he's got to do is pass Officer Basic Course, endure nine months of flight training, spend another three months transitioning to a particular model of helicopter, then survive the inevitable deployment to Iraq, where since the invasion, more than fifty Army helicopters have been destroyed and more than a dozen aviators killed.

One thing at a time, right?

Honestly, Coe's not worried. Statistics are on his side. For as many helicopters that crash, for as many aviators that die or lose limbs, many more choppers complete their missions with no injuries to the crew. Sure, the Army's dangerous. But so is the city of Columbia, which in 2003 had the seventeenth highest violent crime rate of all American cities: 1,100 incidents per 100,000 population versus only 700 for New York City. In fact, the annual death rate of 600 per 100,000 soldiers deployed to Iraq and Afghanistan compares favorably to the rate of 800 for all people living in South Carolina. Coe would rather get shot in Fallujah than shot in Columbia's crime-ridden Eau Claire neighborhood, or compacted in chopper crash than die in a car wreck at the junction of I-26 and I-20.

The Fine Art of Covering Your Ass

While everybody else is shooting at each other in the woods and having epiphanies in the cabins of Blackhawk helicopters, senior business major Wil McLean is worrying about snakes, turned ankles, and, yes, car accidents.

McLean is the battalion S-2, the MSIV in charge of planning—and the human face of the boring half of ROTC. Every week he stands before the Gamecock Battalion's commanding officer—in 2003 a red-faced combat vet colonel named Lewis Buchanan—and briefs him on the week's activities. One of the most important parts of the briefing is the risk assessment, where McLean imagines all the things that could possibly go wrong and how to keep them from happening. Risk assessments are simultaneously the dullest, most serious, and most hilarious part of Army planning. On paper, a risk assessment for an ROTC field training exercise looks something like this:

RISK	RISK LEVEL	CONTROL
Dehydration	High	Drink water
Snake bite	Low	Don't touch the wildlife
Turned ankle	Medium	Look where you're going
Bugs	Low	Wear repellent
Traffic	High	Look both ways
Poisoning	Medium	Don't eat the berries

It's all common sense, of course, but so is almost everything else in the Army. Honestly, even the dumbest freshman cadet knows better than to handle snakes and play in roads. But knowing better and acting on it are two different things, so eventually some gung ho, eighteen-year-old physical education major is going to eat the yummy berries, pet the cute snapping turtle, or chase a stray practice grenade into the road. And when that happens, somebody's going to have to answer to the powers that be.

An important skill of any leader is covering your own ass. And while the Army more than most institutions demands that the guy in charge take responsibility for everything that goes wrong on his watch, when your organization is composed of a hundred college kids, it's wise to have your defense ready in advance. You've got be able to say, "We warned 'em."

So before every holiday, the cadet battalion commander, McLean's classmate and boss, gathers everyone together and gives them the same little speech.

"Be safe, get plenty of rest, and do your homework. Don't drink. But if you do, get a designated driver. Don't have sex. But if you do, use protection. Please take care of yourself. Hooah?"

"Hooah." It's the Army's generic and inexplicable interjection. It's an adjective and even a noun, too. Hooah means "Do you understand?" It also means "yes." You can have a hooah run. You can be a hooah soldier. And if your commander is a little challenged in the vocabulary department, he may call *you* a hooah, as in, "You're the most hooah company of hooahs in the hooah Army! Hooah?"

"Hooah!"

There's just one thing that hooah definitely doesn't mean, and that's "no." So when the cadet battalion commander warns everyone to behave themselves and tells them to come home safely, he expects an enthusiastic hooah in response. And gets one.

There are unspoken prohibitions in addition to the warnings:

Don't do drugs.

Don't be gay.

Avoid radical philosophies.

Don't get involved in politics.

And please, don't criticize the Army, especially to the press.

In 2004, when the situation in Iraq begins to turn south and the media start asking questions, Cadet Command issues "public affairs guidance" to all ROTC units. The twenty-eight-page document advises cadets and cadre to be wary of reporters and even provides stock responses to potential questions:

Q: Should the United States have taken military action against Iraq?

A: Our national leaders must decide the question of whether or not the United States should take military action. It would clearly be inappropriate of me to attempt to second-guess them.

Other "suggested responses" circumvent questions about the draft, prison-abuse scandals, and gays and lesbians in the military. A handy guide appended to the suggested responses tells cadets and cadre exactly what not to do in an interview, such as argue, express anger or sarcasm, speculate, joke, or let the reporter put words in your mouth. A chilling section of the guidance warns cadre about potential protests on campus:

> In the current climate, we cannot rule out the possibility of campus protests impacting on our scheduled awareness and recruiting events. Remain sensitive to this issue and inform us if you foresee the likelihood of a Cadet Command . . . event becoming a target for protestors. Given the sensitive nature of this topic, it is important that our intent in this matter is clearly understood. There is no expectation that you conduct extensive research or enlist the help of others in learning the plans of those who may be contemplating a protest.

In other words, there's no need to spy. Just warn the Army if things start to get tense.

Like they do at Binghamton University in New York in March, when a dozen students gather outside the ROTC building with signs and a boom-box blaring Metallica. Someone reads the names of military casualties through a megaphone. Other protestors form a mock funeral procession and march with an empty coffin draped in an American flag. Still others apply fake blood to their chests and faces and lie in the street feigning death.

Or like at the University of Puerto Rico in February, where thirty students storm an ROTC building and stage a daylong sit-in. Or at MIT in March, where six hundred students march through campus to protest the war in Iraq, ROTC, and what one grad student calls "the military-industrial complex" at the school. Perhaps the most vehement protest takes place at the University of California, Berkeley, in March 2003, on the eve of war. Such is the tenor of the protestors' rhetoric that the ROTC cadre tells Berkeley cadets not to wear their uniforms, lest they make themselves targets.

The war in Iraq pits protestors against ROTC in a way not seen since the '60s. But not at USC, a veritable bastion of conservatism as far as universities go. So it's not protest that worries McLean. Tonight his concerns are of a practical nature. Out in the field, his priority is ending the day with as many cadets as he started it.

It's no easy task.

There's a joke sergeants love to tell: What's the most dangerous thing in the Army? Give up?

A lieutenant with a compass.

There's another: You can't spell "lost" without "Lt."

Green lieutenants are, after all, the last people you should trust to get you anywhere. It's not that they're stupid. They're just inexperienced and in charge.

But any sergeant who's served a stint as an ROTC instructor knows that there's at least one thing more dangerous, and that's a *cadet* with a compass.

For as inexperienced as your average lieutenant is, your average cadet is even worse. Sure, there's the occasional cadet who used to be an enlisted soldier. A few even moonlight in the Reserve or National Guard. But most are fresh out of high school and still getting used to doing their own laundry and feeding themselves. Put 'em in charge and stand back; there are bound to be fuck-ups.

Marvin Mark, for instance, is completely lost somewhere in the woods in the middle of the night. His squad is trying to get to point B from point A. The trick for leaders in situations like this is to keep it simple. Find yourself on the map, figure out the compass direction to your destination, and just walk on that bearing, deviating not an inch in either direction, until you literally run into wherever you're going. It's easy enough in the daylight. But at night, with the trees closing in and the darkness so complete that you can't see your hand in front of your face, point B seems damn near unattainable.

What's more, you've got ten cadets following you. In the darkness, each cadet is supposed to follow the glowing green strips on the cap of the cadet ahead of him in line. But those little green strips are notoriously fickle. Hell, they're *designed* to be hard to see so as not to make easy targets for snipers. Blink and they might disappear. So it's no surprise that somebody in Mark's squad lost track of the cadet in front of him. When that happened he panicked and strayed, throwing off the next person in line, who then lost the person behind him, and so on and so forth. Just a few seconds ago, there were ten cadets all in a line. Now there are little clusters of two or three standing around swearing under their breaths and getting a little nervous.

Fortunately this is not the first time a cadet has gotten lost in the woods. In Marvin Mark's Army there's a plan for every contingency, especially this one. The squad leader gathers together everyone in sight and starts walking in expanding concentric circles. Every few yards they run into somebody and gather them up. Before too long they happen upon Mark leaning against a tree fast asleep.

"Marvin!"

Soon they're all together and, for the time being, not lost. Eventually they return to their platoon's patrol base for a little shut-eye.

It's not unlike camping, but there are key differences. Experienced campers would never go anywhere so poorly equipped. Every cadet's got a rucksack full of socks, T-shirts, and toiletries. In one of their rucksacks' bigger pockets they carry bulky, moth-eaten sleeping bags. Tied under the top flap is what the Army calls a "Matt, Sleeping"—an anemic foam pad intended to provide a buffer between the earth and the all-too-thin sleeping bag. All of this equipment is antiquated by civilian standards. It's heavy, unwieldy, not at all water-resistant, and useless in anything but temperate weather.

But hey, no one ever promised the Army would be comfortable. Besides, after days of pretend combat and hours of wandering half-lost through Fort

Jackson's creepy moonlit woods, Mark is exhausted. He settles into his bag atop his Matt, Sleeping, checks to make sure his rifle is on safety, and falls fast asleep cradling his M16 like a teddy bear. And he dreams of the guns, maps, heavy rucksacks, square women in green uniforms, and bad food.

Which is something he's all too familiar with. If you think college cafeteria fare is fatty and artificial, you haven't indulged in a Meal Ready to Eat, the Army's prepackaged combat rations. MREs come vacuum sealed in impenetrable plastic bags containing impenetrable plastic bags. In each little bag is a food item: spaghetti, maybe, or potatoes with cheese, or a brownie. Ideally you'd use an included chemical heater and a little water to nuke the grub, before dousing it in Tabasco to make it palatable. Unfortunately you tend to eat MREs on the go, so there isn't much time for finesse. Just slice open the less offensive items and pour them right down your gullet. Then pocket the chemical heater and, when you get home, crumble the reagent into a two-liter bottle then fill with water, seal, and throw. The chemical reaction will explode the bottle like a plastic water grenade. They call it an MRE bomb, and it's by the far the best thing to come of the Meal Ready to Eat. In his dreams, Mark throws MRE bombs at cadre and laughs and laughs as they dance around the exploding bottles.

Then he hears a voice saying his name for the second time tonight. And he feels someone touching his shoulder.

"Wake up, damn it."

He opens his eyes. A cadet is crouched over him. His breath freezes in frosty clouds when he exhales. "It's your turn to pull security," he says.

Mark groans and rolls over. Shifting disturbs the fragile cocoon of warmth his body and second-rate sleeping bag have conspired to create. Cold seeps in.

He climbs out of his bag with his rifle. The other cadet barely hesitates. In seconds he's deep in his own sleeping bag, sighing in relief. For the next hour, Mark is the platoon's only security. He's supposed to walk the perimeter, investigate suspicious activity, and challenge anyone who approaches. If they're friendly, they'll know the prearranged password. If not, they're bad guys, and Mark will take them prisoner or, if he doesn't feel like dealing with a prisoner, just open fire with his blanks and see what happens.

Challenges and passwords are one way the Army has its fun.

Today's challenge is "game" and the password is "cock." But Mark never has the chance to make some poor sleepwalking cadet holler "Cock!" His hour on security passes peacefully, just him, the nocturnal creatures of these South Carolina woods, and the gentle snores and farts of sleeping cadets. Standing under the restless canopy, gazing at the stars and moon and twinkling airplanes passing overhead, Mark thinks about his future.

He's got it all planned out. Graduate with an engineering degree in the fall of 2004. Hopefully get into the Army's Signal Branch. Go to Officer Basic Course, then take command of a platoon. What with the war in Iraq underway and a long occupation inevitable, Mark is sure to get deployed. But that's all part of being an officer. When he gets back, he'll be a first lieutenant. After a couple years and another deployment, he'll make captain. Then major. Then lieutenant colonel. By then he'll have twenty years in the service and be eligible for retirement.

It's like clockwork, the Army is. The major decisions are all up-front. After that, options and surprises get increasingly rare. The biggest decision is joining the Army in the first place; the next is your branch. Every branch has its schools and routines and expectations. Unless you're some high-speed superstar and end up divorcing your branch for Special Forces or Delta Force, nobody much deviates. Even Special Forces has habits.

Steady. Predictable. Businesslike. Nothing can rattle the U.S. Army because it's designed and equipped to cope with chaos. Even war's perfectly routine to the U.S. Army, especially after September 11.

And that's exactly how Marvin Mark likes it. He didn't join ROTC to make friends. He didn't join for fun and excitement. He didn't join because he likes the pretty uniforms. He joined because being an Army officer's a good job with good benefits. It's challenging. It's interesting. It's good solid work. And for a black southerner like Mark, it's a step up in the world.

The racial factor makes the Gamecock Battalion unique. A quarter of its eighty cadets are black, whereas only 12 percent of the Army's officers are black. Speaking a year and a half later at a commissioning ceremony in August 2004, Col. Jack Collins, himself a black man, turns to the four graduating cadets, all of whom are African Americans.

"This isn't in my speech," he says, "but just let me say, I'm proud of you, for you represent a rare breed. We need African American officers in our force."

He's right. But the reverse is also true. African Americans need the Army, too. In the United States in 2004, half of all black men between the ages of sixteen and twenty-two are out of work, according to a conference of black congressmen. The same conference finds that 87 percent of juvenile parolees and 60 percent of adult parolees are black. According to the Department of Justice, 12.9 percent of black men between twenty-five and twenty-nine are in prison or jail in 2004, more than ten times the rate for whites.

African Americans are in a crisis. They need good careers like they need oxygen. It's a matter of survival.

Mark knows that sooner or later he's going to war. It doesn't scare him. By the time he graduates, a thousand Americans have died in Iraq. But statistically speaking, the Iraqi war zone is safer for black men than America is. Nobody knows this better than Willie Martin, one of Mark's classmates. Just a couple days after standing before Colonel Collins and swearing his oath to defend the constitution, et cetera, one of Martin's good friends is killed. The dead young man was in his early twenties.

Joining the Army and going to war is just about the smartest thing Mark and his black classmates can do. It's smart for a lot of people, regardless of race, especially if they're single. McLean graduates in May and promptly ships out to Fort Benning, Georgia, for a couple years of advanced training before deploying to Iraq in early 2005. He's looking forward to it, for financial reasons at least. A second lieutenant in the U.S. Army makes around $25,000 year in base pay. Add to that a monthly housing allowance and other benefits, including free health care, cheap insurance, and discount shopping at military post exchanges. Benefits included, a lieutenant pulls in more than $30,000. And it gets even better in a war zone, where he's eligible for combat pay. What's more, deployed soldiers pay no taxes and, if they're single, have essentially no expenses. McLean might return from an eighteen-month deployment with $50,000 burning a hole in his pocket. And if he doesn't return, if he takes a bullet or catches a bug or gets blown to bits by a roadside bomb, his parents will collect a couple hundred grand in life insurance.

Considering that many ROTC cadets go to school on Army scholarships, few graduate with much in the way of student-loan debt. Out of the gate, cadets are way ahead of their civilian peers, the average of whom carries a debt of $15,000 coming out of college. In the weak, post–September 11 economy, junior officers actually make more money than their civilian counterparts. Who knew war could be such good business?

Sophomore John Thorne, that's who. For Thorne, the Army's just a job and a part-time one at that. Don't get him wrong, he likes the Army. But he's got a wife and a career in life insurance. He's twenty-four years old and a sergeant in a reserve military police company. And for the last four years he's been cobbling together a business degree at Midlands Technical College, one of the small local schools that sends its cadets to USC for training. Thorne joined ROTC because lieutenant's bars mean a better work environment and better pay: six hundred dollars more per month, to be exact.

Thorne's the old man of ROTC. But despite his years of experience at home and overseas, in 2003 he's just a sophomore cadet and not even the best of his class. He's been there, done that, and it's hard to get excited about drill and ceremony and squad tactics when he's been doing them for five years. Nor is Thorne the best at PT. While hardly old by any rational standard, he's no glorified high school kid fresh off the varsity track team. His knees creak just a little sometimes. And he has no patience for patriotism and all that.

Since 2001 Thorne's MP unit has been in high demand. He's done stints in Bosnia and Cuba, and in 2004 he gets tapped for duty in Iraq. If he's going to spend half his time away from the wife and the insurance biz wrangling terrorists and thugs for the U.S. government, he's going to do it on an officer's salary and with an officer's perks.

Other cadets' motivations for joining the Army are less practical.

For some, it all began the first time they saw a soldier in his dress uniform. For others, it was a visit with a recruiter or a sit-down with a guidance counselor that made the difference. For still others, it was when they saw that glossy pamphlet with ROTC on the outside and the words "money for college" on the inside.

For a few it was September 11.

But for Wil McLean, there was never a day when he decided to join the Army. It was always a foregone conclusion, one he was perfectly comfortable with.

McLean is a weirdo. Most USC cadets are from South Carolina, and like all good South Carolinians, their identities are rooted in the dirt and the sky, the woods they played in as kids, the small towns with big churches and bigger high schools where they grew up, places like Darlington and Aiken and Cheraw. Ask Jonathan Coe where he's from and he'll tell you. Ask senior Jennifer Fauth, she'll do the same. But ask McLean and he stutters and blinks. The question doesn't make sense to him. The son of a career soldier, he's lived just about everywhere the Army takes a man: North Carolina, Kentucky, Louisiana, Panama, and a few places he can't remember. His accent reflects his regional rootlessness: it sounds like a little bit of everywhere. Like any Army brat, McLean learned to adapt to wherever he found himself. So when his dad retired in Columbia to be near Fort Jackson, with its massive post exchange, nearby veteran's hospitals, and huge community of military veterans, it was natural for McLean to apply to USC for college and just as natural for him to accept an Army ROTC scholarship. He never even considered applying for any of the other branches. At USC, they're all offered: Navy, Marine Corps, and Air Force. But being in the Navy would have been like visiting a foreign country.

To McLean the Army isn't just a paycheck. It's not just a passion either. It's home.

Minus the Laugh Track 5

There's a great irony at work in the U.S. military: one of the most fearsome fighting forces the world has ever known is also one of the silliest. The Army even has its own term for silliness: "grab-ass." In 2003 and '04, with two hundred thousand Americans in war zones in Afghanistan and Iraq, tales of international grab-ass abound.

There's the Marine captain from Illinois whose unit captured a Soviet-made tank in Baghdad in April 2003. A self-described gearhead with a stated goal of driving every motorized vehicle in the Defense Department inventory, the officer got a crash course in tank operation from one of his soldiers, a corporal from South Carolina, then took the antiquated T-72 for a spin around the company area. Only when he started to worry that coalition forces might mistake him for an Iraqi counterattack did he reluctantly park the tank and emerge happy, flushed, and one vehicle closer to achieving his goal.

Then there are the soldiers from the 101st Airborne Division who, after capturing one of Saddam's palaces overlooking the ruins of Babylon, celebrated with a dip in the Euphrates River—naked. It was their first moment of freedom since crossing the border into Iraq, a chance to relax after two weeks of combat. That water was probably pretty dirty: sanitation standards in Iraq were low after a decade of sanctions. So everybody was careful to keep their mouths closed and above water.

And of course there are the jokers of the 372nd Military Police Company, an Army Reserve unit from Maryland, who stacked Iraqi prisoners in pyramids, stripped them naked, chased them around with dogs, and took hundreds of photos to show to their friends. Anyone who thinks the Abu Ghraib incident is exceptional doesn't know the U.S. military. It's not that soldiers and Marines are bad people or even mean people. It's just that their definition of fun doesn't always jibe with everyone else's.

Perhaps worse, in many cases the typical soldier's sensibilities *do* jibe with those of the average American, which is why American soldiers love foul-mouthed black comedians, bad-assed white rap-rockers, beer, NASCAR, and cheesy action movies. Inasmuch as American popular culture is drunken, violent, narcissistic, and profane, the U.S. Army is, too.

But there's another side to the coin. For every race car–loving, beer-swilling redneck soldier there's a National Public Radio addict with an indie pop collection and a penchant for IKEA. There are hard-core Christian soldiers, left-leaning liberal types, and aviators who harbor a secret love for Tom Cruise in *Top Gun.* There are gay soldiers, lesbian soldiers, bisexuals, transvestites, and soldiers who think the aforementioned are all going to hell. America's a big place and its people are diverse. The U.S. Army, a million strong and growing, is just as diverse.

ROTC is, too. The Gamecock Battalion in 2004 numbers around eighty cadets and a dozen cadre and staff. There are around sixty men and twenty women. Twenty-five are black, fifty are white, and the rest Hispanic or "other." While most cadets hail from South Carolina, others are from Virginia and Pennsylvania and elsewhere. Their personalities vary wildly.

Sophomore Joe Crumpton was the shy, nerdy type until he pledged Alpha Phi Alpha and turned into a hard-partying frat boy with a goofy streak.

Neil Truslow, a sophomore and the son of a career Army officer, came into ROTC with a four-year scholarship and a lifetime of living on Army bases. He thinks he knows everything about everything, and in some cases he's right. Truslow looks great in uniform and knows how to make a good impression, but less flashy cadets resent him. To them, he's a Blue Falcon, a derogatory euphemism for "buddy-fucker." Blue Falcons are great soldiers when the commander's watching. But they'll screw you in a heartbeat when nobody else is around.

A Nigerian-born senior cadet named Omololu Makinde is a legendary PT stud, worshipped by younger cadets and envied by his peers for his ability to run seemingly effortless five-minute miles.

Junior Jennifer Fauth is a model of professionalism and courtesy. Liked by all and feared by some, she seems destined for rank and responsibility. And boy can she drink. Many Thursdays you can find her at Delaney's pub in Five Points. Fauth is the one sitting under the stage where the Scottish folksinger strums bar tunes with a wry smile. She's got a little blue card listing every beer in the house. As she tries one, she marks it off the list. If she completes the card she gets a free T-shirt. Getting that free shirt is important to Fauth, and not because she needs shirts. Drinking is a mission and the T-shirt is the objective. When it comes to missions, military or otherwise, Fauth doesn't know the meaning of failure.

Sophomore Daniel Rowland, on the other hand, doesn't give a damn about missions. He just wants to eat bugs, roll in the mud, and haul machine guns through the woods. The Gamecock Battalion's token John Rambo, Rowland once got caught wearing a red bandana on an FTX. He was using it to secure foliage to his head—mobile camouflage, he said, only half-joking.

And of course there's McLean, the recent graduate who wears his love for the Army like a halo or the mark of the beast. And Coe, the slight, quiet, wannabe aviator who some suspect is scared of the dark.

Last but not least, there's a gabby freshman named Kim Griggs. She carries two cell phones, one in each pocket, because she loves the idea of getting lost, and sometimes that terrifies her. Her cell phones are her way of making sure she stays in touch with the world, even when she doesn't want to.

In many ways Griggs is an outsider. A Pennsylvania-born Yankee, an African American, a devout Christian, and a woman, in the Gamecock Battalion she's a minority within a minority within a minority within a minority. Which is fine by her. She came to South Carolina because, by her standards, it's a wilderness: deep, wide, and unknowable. She's a walking, talking contradiction, a friendly, ambitious young woman helplessly in love with hardship and anonymity. And despite her impatience with bullshit, she's got an active imagination. When she looks around at her peers and superiors in the Gamecock Battalion, she sees not budding junior officers and their longsuffering trainers, but the cast of a naturalistic television comedy with a military setting—an Army sitcom minus the laugh track.

How else can you explain Master Sgt. Dan Bell, a mustachioed Special Forces veteran with so many colorful medals and badges that his green dress uniform looks like a garden? With his pointy nose, beady eyes, toothy grin, and growing paunch, Bell looks nothing like the stereotypical lean, mean commandoes in movies. If anything, he looks like a used-car salesman or a door-to-door vacuum peddler. He acts like one too, always slouching and sniggering when he's not strutting around for show. When Sergeant Blaylock caught Rowland with the bandana on his head, Bell put on his most furious expression and bellowed, "Damn it, Rowland, you've got it on crooked!"

Or what about Lt. Col. John Moring, the prototypical compassionate father figure in the vein of 1950s TV shows if there ever was one. Moring's got the weathered face of a man who knows what he's talking about, an easy smile that assures you everything's going to be okay, and this circuitous way of talking that's simultaneously annoying and hypnotic. He says things like, "I'm proud, very proud, of what you've done and what you've accomplished."

Moring was a high school teacher and basketball coach in Texas before he enlisted in the Army in 1982. He went through basic training at Fort Jackson, coincidentally, and eventually got his commission through Officer Candidates

School. Moring was an infantry officer for four years before transferring to military intelligence. After serving in Korea and Europe, he landed back in the States as commander of all Army recruiting in South Carolina and western North Carolina. When that gig ended, the ROTC position opened up, and Moring made his move. It's perfect for a guy like him, someone with years of experience in recruiting and the kind of attitude that endears him to college kids and stuffy academics.

Besides, he's always wanted to get back into teaching. As professor of military science and chair of his department, Moring teaches courses in military history, tradition, and ethics. And he loves every minute.

If Moring is the affable, slightly absent-minded, Ward Cleaver sort of patriarch, then his immediate predecessor, Lewis Buchanan, is the opposite: hard, aggressive, and a little bit frightening, a father figure in the vein of Dan Lauria's character Jack Arnold from *The Wonder Years*. Buchanan took a no-bullshit approach to training. He didn't let anything distract from his main purpose in life, which was preparing the next generation of Army officers for combat. To that end he did all he could to expose cadets to "real" Army experiences, like short hops in Blackhawk helicopters. When Moring took over in 2003, he put an end to the chopper rides. Too dangerous, he said. Never mind that by September 2004, ninety officers have died in Iraq. Never mind that just being in the Army is dangerous. Moring sees his job as protecting cadets from harm and distraction so they can focus on what he feels really matters: their educations. If that means that at times ROTC training seems a little toothless, then so be it.

Basing a military training unit on the campus of a civilian university means all sorts of concessions for the sake of safety and decorum. While some ROTC units have their own arms rooms, USC has a no-firearms policy, so the Gamecock Battalion borrows its weapons from Fort Jackson. Even the battalion's use of fake weapons—"rubber duckies"—is restricted. Duckies look and feel just like real M16s, and the sight of a ducky in the hands of a young man with a shaved head is enough to cause a general panic, as it did on April 8, 2003, when a USC ROTC cadet on a road march with a ducky prompted a flurry of phone calls to the campus cops by frightened undergrads, who were convinced that their campus was under siege à la Columbine. The poor cadet found himself surrounded by a small army of campus cops while he rather unconvincingly explained himself. Sans laugh track, the episode was more chilling than humorous.

There are times when Griggs wishes the Gamecock Battalion were *more* like a sitcom. In sitcoms there's always a buzz of activity. Everyone knows everyone. Sure, there are conflicts, but they're conflicts born of relationships, not of a lack of them. Sitcoms are never lonely. For Griggs, ROTC often is.

Frats are part of the problem. What little free time they do have after homework and training, many male cadets devote to their fraternities. And inasmuch as *they* frequent frat parties, so do some of the females. Griggs is proud of her independence; she hates the idea of buying friends with fraternity dues. She's also a light drinker. She quickly tires of cadets' penchant for alcohol-soaked parties.

But what parties they are. Hardly a week goes by that someone doesn't announce a get-together at their duplex, apartment, or the house their daddy pays for. Sometimes it's Mitch Monroe, the tan-skinned, bleached-blonde fresh-man from Virginia. Other times it's Makinde or sophomore Patrick Gillespie, the honorary social chairs of ROTC. Sometimes they throw toga parties, where everyone stumbles around in sheets and boxer shorts, ogling and groping each other, and burping up beer.

Toga parties are the exception, and a distraction from the real purpose of week-ends and Thursday nights, which is drinking, just drinking. When it comes to ROTC socials, usually somebody just ponies up some cash for booze—beer, wine coolers, liquor, whatever—then everybody sits around and plays drinking games.

Games like "Circle of Death." The rules are complicated, and after a drink or two, Griggs has no idea what's going on. Circle of Death seems to involve pulling cards from a deck and, depending on the card's suit and value, drink-ing or making other people drink. All she knows is that everyone ends up wasted, even that Jerry Banfield kid, who's notoriously professional when it comes to boozing. Pretty soon, Sawyer and Young are stealing people's clothes and making makeshift togas out of them. Everyone's laughing and tripping over each other. There are a lot of smiles and flushed faces. But for all the gid-diness, Griggs just doesn't feel much love.

This isn't happiness. It's unhappiness on drugs. And it gets worse. At one party, everybody decides to go to Platinum Plus, a popular strip club. Griggs has second thoughts. But when everyone heads out the door and the empty apartment begins to close in around her, she changes her mind. For safety's sake, she sidles up to Fauth and one of Fauth's female friends. At the club, the men are drinking, hollering, and using their ROTC stipends to buy lap dances from coked-out strippers. Meanwhile Fauth's friend has had a few and is start-ing to get a little amorous towards Griggs. And while Griggs is many things, a lesbian she is not. There are some areas where Griggs and the Army don't see eye to eye, but the Army's stance on homosexuality is not one of them. Griggs knows there are gays and lesbians out there. She just doesn't want to see them or hear about them.

It's time to go, she decides. Some things are worse than loneliness. Besides, Griggs has been lonely for a long time, despite a constant parade of suitors, including a man at her church and the Gamecock Battalion's civilian supply tech, both of whom have a couple decades on Griggs but just didn't under-stand why it couldn't work out. It's tough to say who was worse. Supply guy put a down payment on a ring for her even though he's married. And the dude from church made friends with Griggs's estranged father and even volunteered to drive him down from Pennsylvania to see her, just to get on her good side. Griggs even dated Makinde for a while. But when he figured out that she was a virgin and intended to stay that way, he sort of lost interest.

The kind of company the men in her life offer is not the kind she wants. Griggs wants to spend more time with her peers: people her age, with her interests, who want more than to sleep with her. She wants to spend time with other cadets outside of labs, PT, and FTXs, and not just to drink and debauch. She wants ROTC to be less like a frat, less like a hedonistic celebration of the impending apocalypse, and more like a family. A *healthy* family.

After all, the *real* Army's one big family, right?

Moring agrees with Griggs. He knows about the drinking, and he knows it's not doing anybody any good. So another change he institutes after taking over from Buchanan is to clean out an old supply room in the military science building and convert it into a cadet lounge with sofas. He even budgets for a big-screen TV.

Call it grab-ass central. The idea is that cadets hang out there, under the semiwatchful eyes of the cadre.

For much of her freshman year, Griggs's home away from home is the lounge. It's like the living room of her imagined sitcom family, a place where folks are always coming and going. It's here in the cadet lounge that Griggs makes friends with Fauth. It's here that Griggs overhears the gossip and rumors and private conversations that make her superiors and peers into three-dimensional characters, heroes and villains alike.

Like Sergeant Aiken, the muscular, balding black man with his own Internet business and a thirteen-year-old daughter who is slowly dying of cancer. Lately the girl has been getting worse: she can't get comfortable and she can't sleep. Which means Aiken can't sleep either. He's used to getting a couple hours per night. Now he's lucky to get any. He just drinks coffee, keeps moving, smiles at his cadets, and tells himself and everyone else that everything is going to be okay. To Griggs, Sergeant Aiken is one of the heroes of the Gamecock Battalion, a good soldier who also manages to be a good man.

Not all the cadre are good men. Like the NCO from one of the satellite schools who sexually harasses all the female cadets. One time at an FTX, the sergeant even threatened a female cadet, saying he'd make her life miserable if she ever told anyone he'd been harassing her.

It happened like this: After shooting at the Fort Jackson firing range, everyone is thoroughly frisked to make sure they're not carrying any ammo or casings, both of which are highly controlled items in the Army. Men frisk men and women frisk women. This one female cadet just happened to have some candy in her pockets, so she removed it all before getting patted down. "No brass, no ammo," she said. And sure enough, she was right. Cleared by her female inspector, the cadet started slipping candy back into her pockets. The NCO saw her—and saw his opportunity. On the pretext of making sure it wasn't ammo she was returning to her pocket, the sergeant got into the girl's face and started patting her legs. Noting the cadet's nervous smile, he coined a little nickname for her: "Smiley."

"You know what you need, Smiley?" he said. "You need to get laid. Maybe I'll do something about that."

The cadet freaked out. She looked around for Sergeant Blaylock, the one guy she could count on to save her. But Blaylock had just caught a cadet smuggling a condom in his pocket and was currently somewhere private, giving the cadet the ass-chewing of a lifetime.

Her savior indisposed, the poor, harassed cadet just grinned and bore it. Soon enough the sergeant got jumpy and moved on to his next victim. Before he did he hissed, "If you ever tell anyone, I'll make the next four years a living hell for you."

Sitting in the lounge shooting the shit with the other females, Griggs hears more horror stories just like this. Maybe ROTC isn't a sitcom after all. Maybe it's an after-school special or a Lifetime Original Movie. God forbid that it should be anything with real adult content. Institutionalized violence, tactical training, and marksmanship are okay. This is America. We *thrive* on graphic violence. But scenes of rape . . . unacceptable. And perhaps inevitable if things don't change in the Gamecock Battalion.

And so it's here in the cadet lounge that Griggs begins to position herself as the dominant offspring of the Gamecock Battalion's dysfunctional TV family. She's going to be the main character, the battalion commander. And she's going to change things. No more binge drinking. No more lesbian come-ons. No more sexual harassment. The Gamecock Battalion will be a happier, safer place.

Easier said than done, of course. How she gets from lonely little freshman to respected senior and leader of her peers is anyone's guess.

Actually, she has a plan. And a key part of it is something called Ranger Challenge.

Ranger Challenged 6

On the morning of June 6, 1944, two hundred American commandoes packed into flimsy landing craft plied through the English Channel towards the imposing cliffs of Pointe-du-Hoc, a German strongpoint on the Normandy coast.

The commandoes were called Rangers, five battalions of whom had been raised in 1942 as an experiment based on British experience with specially trained elite infantry. Two Ranger battalions, each with about four hundred men, were taking part in the Allied assault on Normandy. While their brethren churned towards Pointe-du-Hoc, the rest of the Rangers hurled themselves ashore at Omaha Beach with a couple hundred troops from a regular infantry regiment. When everybody got bogged down under murderous fire, a general famously said, "I'm counting on you Rangers to lead the way."

And so they did.

Meanwhile, the Rangers at Pointe-du-Hoc hit the beach, scaled the cliffs with bayonets and ropes, and took out German fortifications on the top. Half of the Rangers were killed or wounded, but they accomplished their mission and gave birth to a legend.

Sixty years later a regiment of Rangers based at Fort Benning is the sharp point of the Army's light infantry force and the core of the entire Army ethos. Drill sergeants tell stories about Rangers as examples to new recruits. Men join Infantry just to get a shot at Ranger School. "Rangers lead the way," is something you hear not just at Benning, but everywhere a leader is trying to motivate his soldiers. And in 2000 the chief of staff decided to make the traditional Ranger black beret the official headgear of the entire Army, a move designed to boost morale after a decade that saw the Army muck about in the Balkans and squabble internally over what to do with gays and whether to allow women in combat.

Cadet Command was way ahead of the chief of staff. In 1986 it launched a little program it called Ranger Challenge, a two-day competition for cadets emphasizing tactical skills and physical fitness, a sort of varsity sport for Army ROTC.

In 2002 events include the following:

1. Army physical fitness test: A variant of the standard APFT, the Ranger Challenge version of the test features some of the strictest graders this side of drill sergeant's school. There are no half push-ups and fudged sit-ups here. Most cadets end up doing a third more repetitions than the graders award them. In other words, to max out push-ups as a twenty-one-year-old man, you've got to do about a hundred. And the two-mile run? It's on a sandy trail through the woods, and it's uphill most of the way. For the same twenty-one-year-old man, a time of 13:18 gets you the maximum score.

2. Grenade assault course: An event in which cadets navigate obstacles to lob training grenades at plastic targets. The grenades look and feel just like the real thing, but instead of exploding when you pull the pin and flip the handle, they just fizzle and pop. The obstacle course requires cadets to crawl on their bellies ("low crawl"), scoot along on their elbows ("high crawl"), and scale a short wall. Grenades are thrown from kneeling and prone positions, and points are awarded for form and accuracy. And be careful not to lose a grenade. That little faux pas will cost you dearly.

3. Weapon assembly: Cadets sprint fifty yards to a station, where a grader watches them disassemble and reassemble an M16 then perform a functions check and sprint back. Points are based on time. Fast weaponeers are known to complete the event in thirty seconds.

4. Day land navigation: Forty points are scattered on a four-square-mile course. Teams break up into four buddy pairs; each pair goes after ten points. The team to find all forty points fastest wins the event. Considering the distance between the points and the speed required to win, land navigation is like running a very precise four-mile race through the woods.

5. Rope bridge: Teams must cross an obstacle between two posts using only one long rope, as well as a short rope and a D-ring for each team member. The idea is to tie the short rope in harness around your midsection then string the long rope between the posts. Cadets hook their harnesses to the long rope by way of the D-ring and pull themselves across the obstacle. Winning teams accomplish all of this in around two minutes.

6. Marksmanship: One M16. One magazine. One target, twenty-five meters downrange. Every shot counts. The closer you get to hitting the man-shaped target "center mass" (that is, in the heart), the more points you score.

7. Patrolling exam: A paper exam testing knowledge of Field Manual 7-8, the infantry bible. What is the effective range of an M60? How do you clear a

jammed rifle? How do you silently signal to your squad to watch out for booby traps? You're expected to know all of this and more.

8. Road march: Teams run a hilly six-mile course with full rucksacks and weapons, ending on the parade ground where the closing ceremony takes place. Everybody in the team must stay together; leave behind a teammate and you're disqualified. After all, it's in the Ranger credo: "Never will I leave a fallen comrade."

With the possible exception of the patrolling exam, every event is more difficult than anything the average cadet will face in four years without Ranger Challenge. Simply put, it's the hardest thing you can do in ROTC. People bleed. People hurt. People cry.

Which is why Ranger Challenge is strictly voluntary. Most ROTC units field only one team, but some field as many as three. Each team of nine is led by one of the toughest, smartest cadets in the battalion, who is usually elected by his or her peers, bestowed with the honorary title "Ranger Daddy" or "Ranger Momma," and practically worshipped. Most teams train every day through the fall semester. Some train year-round. They're authorized to wear special patches, custom T-shirts, and (until they were adopted Army-wide) black berets. And they're given license to act a little cockier than the average cadet.

And if they happen to win a regional or national title, they can act even cockier. Victorious Ranger Challenge teams bring honor and attention to their host units and tend to aid recruiting. Who doesn't want to be a part of the meanest ROTC unit in the country?

Plenty of people, that's who. Ranger Challenge may pale in comparison to Ranger School or the Ranger Regiment or anything in the "real" Army, for that matter. But by ROTC standards, it's hard-core. And it's a litmus test for cadets. There are those who eagerly volunteer for Ranger Challenge team. And there are those who avoid it like the plague. Needless to say, it's the Ranger Challenge cadets who score Airborne slots, serve as battalion commander, and end up in branches like Aviation and Infantry. Ranger Challenge proves to the Army that maybe, just maybe, you have what it takes to be a real soldier and not just some "rear-echelon motherfucker," or REMF, one of the Army's many derogatory terms for soldiers who don't habitually get shot at.

Real Rangers—that is, soldiers who have been through the fifty-eight-day Ranger School at Fort Benning and who have earned the right to wear the vaunted Ranger tab on their left shoulders—don't see things the way Cadet Command does. They're known to be a little jealous of their name. Some don't like a bunch of ROTC cadets appropriating it. So it's wise when you head to Airborne School or Advanced Camp to take the Ranger Challenge tabs off your uniform, lest some twenty-year veteran of a Ranger battalion see it and unkindly remove it for you, often by ripping it right off your shoulder and leaving a long gash in your sleeve. To those who think their Army is the "real" Army, ROTC is a gaggle of pretenders, and Ranger Challenge their poseur flagship.

But to Coe, Ranger Challenge is a chance to experience just a little of that legendary real Army. It's like boot camp in little spurts. For two months, they PT five days per week with Major Nelson—himself a real live Ranger—doing sit-ups till they puke and push-ups till they cry and running till their legs are like rubber. On Saturdays they practice events, throwing hundreds of dummy grenades, stringing up countless rope bridges, poring over maps, and wandering all over campus to get familiar with the Army's antiquated compasses, which haven't changed much in fifty years. Coe and his teammates' training schedule for the 2002 competition looks something like this:

On Mondays, run five or six miles then head to the pull-up bars for a "pyramid"—that is, six sets of decreasing reps. Twelve then ten then eight then six, four, three, for a total of forty-three damn pull-ups in the space of a few minutes.

Wednesday, do push-ups until your muscles fail. For most people that works out to around three hundred repetitions.

Friday's easy, relatively speaking. Sprint around the track a few times for a total distance of three miles. Wrap with a few dips and an ab workout, which at the tail end of two road marches and hundreds of push-ups is a veritable vacation.

And a much-needed one. For on Tuesdays and Thursdays, the Gamecocks Rangers wake before dawn to participate in a little something the Army calls a "forced road march."

For many cadets, just running the two miles required by the PT test, and doing it in comfortable shoes and shorts, is hard enough. Now imagine running two or three times that distance, and doing it in combat boots, fatigues, and full canteens in addition to a pack and a rubber ducky—and doing it at 5 A.M., when you're hungry, only half-awake, and stiff from sleep. And you know full well that all your friends who aren't in Ranger Challenge, civilian and ROTC alike, are fast asleep and dreaming of scrambled eggs and bacon.

Road marches—or "ruck runs," as some cadets call them—hurt in ways that Coe has never hurt before. His shins scream, his shoulders pop, and those fucking canteens bounce against his hips until he bruises. And that damn rucksack shifts and bounces and drags until his spine's a pretzel and every muscle in his back threatens to pull right off the bone.

And that's after only a quarter mile.

Make no mistake, road marches suck. But like many things that suck, like final exams and shitty part-time jobs, there's a reward at the end. Ranger Challenge teams road march together, shuffling down the road in a sloppy, single-file line. Everyone suffers. Everyone complains. But it's rare that anyone quits, for to quit is to let down your team, your team that hurts just like you do, that's so tired that thoughts of sleep take on an erotic quality, that's so hungry that the only thing that keeps it going besides camaraderie is the thought of a big, greasy breakfast. The reward is not physical fitness, for road marches cause more physical problems than they solve, problems like back pain, blisters, and bad knees. Nor is the reward monetary or academic, for, if anything, Ranger Challenge PT—and especially road marches—ends up hurting competitors' grades and performances at work.

No, the reward is the euphoria. It starts somewhere near the end of a road march, sometime midway through the training season. It comes from knowing that the finish line is near, but your teammates are nearer. And it comes from knowing that even though your body was never meant to run six miles with a thirty-pound mass on its back, you can force it to do just that, more than once, while wearing an insane, bloodthirsty grin on your face.

The euphoria feels different to everyone. To some it's a tingling sensation. To others it's numbness. To a few it's coupled with an almost religious sense of peace, like your body is recognizing that things simply can't get any worse, so relief must be on the way.

Some cadets swear that they've seen God on road marches, that the heavens opened up and the Creator cast loving beams of grace down on the faces of the suffering supplicant. But not Coe. He's a sensible guy, and he knows that God doesn't favor USC Ranger Challenge.

If he did, the Gamecock Rangers surely would win when they square off against their longtime rival the Citadel at the October 2002 Ranger Challenge competition at Fort Jackson. It's their own turf, and still those Citadel cadets manage to kick USC's asses almost every year.

2002 is no exception.

The Citadel is one of the nation's few remaining senior military colleges, civilian schools organized along martial lines, with uniforms, a rank structure, strict admissions standards, and a long-standing ethos that's one part southern pride and one part religious fundamentalism with dashes of various -isms on top. The Citadel, located in Charleston, South Carolina, made national news in 1995 when it admitted its first female cadet, Shannon Faulkner, who suffered so much that she dropped out after only one week and transferred to Furman University in Greenville. Some say she was out of shape. Others say she was harassed till she broke.

Senior military colleges like Virginia Tech, Virginia Military Institute, and the Citadel enthusiastically embrace ROTC, in most cases playing host to units from all the different branches of the military. Every student is required to join ROTC for two years, and many remain through the end and earn their commissions. If West Point produces the Army's grunts and professional automatons, and civilian schools like USC create the Army's true citizen-soldiers, then senior military colleges graduate bad hybrids of both: reactionary brutes without the benefit of West Point's high standards of professionalism.

And boy do they ever PT at schools like the Citadel. In response to an epidemic of fatigue and falling grades blamed on early-morning workouts in 2004, Citadel's administration publishes new guidelines prohibiting cadets from waking earlier than 5:40 A.M. on the three days per week that they're allowed to PT. But that's just for your average joe; Citadel's Ranger Challenge team trains twice per day and on weekends for a grand total of thirty hours a week. Even USC's team doesn't train *that* hard.

So the Gamecocks lose, year after miserable year.

Which may be one reason why Coe eventually loses interest in Ranger Challenge. It's demoralizing getting beaten every year by seemingly the same bunch of identical buzz-headed white guys. Or maybe Coe's just gotten it out of his system. He's had a taste of the "real" Army. Now he wants his life back. So his senior year he opts out of Ranger Challenge.

Which is fine by Griggs. That opens up a spot on the team for her.

Ambitions aside, it's the camaraderie of Ranger Challenge that Griggs is drawn to. She finds herself one of only two freshmen on the Gamecock Battalion's 2003 Ranger Challenge team, and the only other woman besides Fauth. But rather than feeling like the same old minority within a minority, Griggs feels right at home with the Gamecock Rangers.

It's a diverse and motivated team that USC fields in 2003: a couple of eager freshmen including Griggs, a strong core of juniors like Fauth, and some seasoned seniors, among them a real PT stud named Michael Courtwright, this year's Ranger Daddy. There's a good mix of men and women, an advantage over all-male teams like the Citadel's, considering that women tend to excel in events like land nav and grenade assault, while men are better at road marching and weapons assembly.

In light of female cadets' natural strengths, changes to the competition between 2002 and 2003 give teams with women an even bigger advantage than before.

Gone is the road march. In its place, cadets will be timed as they march from event to event, never more than a mile or two. Gone, too, is marksmanship and the patrolling exam. New this year are a night land nav course, a map-reading exam, an obstacle course, and a wild-card contest called the commander's event. The new roster of events diminishes traditionally "masculine" events in favor of more cerebral "feminine" events.

For the first time circumstances favor USC. Maybe this year's their year. Maybe, finally, the Citadel will fall.

But there are signs that maybe this year *isn't* their year. First of all, USC has a no-guns policy, which means the Gamecock Battalion has to go to Fort Jackson and borrow rifles whenever they want to practice weapons assembly and marksmanship. It's ridiculous that the average gangbanger in the Columbia ghettos has easier access to firearms than the local Army ROTC. Hell, even Furman, a tiny private college, has its own arms room. Their cadets can check out an M16 whenever they want and practice into the wee hours. For the Gamecocks it's a serious challenge.

And there are a couple curious absences from the team. The battalion's biggest PT stud is senior Makinde, and after several years of competition, he's decided to sit this one out.

Signs aside, things go just fine for the 2003 Gamecock Rangers—for a while at least. All nine events take place on a single day on a remote corner of Fort Jackson as a small army of graders and spectators observes. It's like watching a very orderly little war. Even the proverbial "fog of war" is in place. Teams draw their schedules from a hat—and when half the events are all or mostly physical in nature, schedules matter. Nobody wants to do grenade assault, day land nav and night land nav all in row. Thus luck plays a huge role in winning.

The Gamecock's schedule looks like this:

1. APFT (at 4:00 A.M.!)
2. Rope bridge
3. Grenade assault
4. Obstacle course
5. Weapon assembly
6. Day land nav
7. Map reading
8. Commander's event
9. Night land nav

It's perfect. The physically toughest events are separated by little breaks, like map reading and weapon assembly. So the Gamecocks are feeling pretty good going into the rope bridge, typically one of their better events.

Rope bridge is tough: a test of physical strength, skill with knots, and, above all, teamwork. In theory it's simple: get everybody from one end of muddy pit to the other. In practice it's a little more complicated. Only two cadets can actually enter the obstacle. The others have to cross on the bridge. And don't forget, it's a race.

When the grader says, "Go!" Fauth grabs an end of the long rope and plows through the mud to the far shore, where she wraps her end around a tall post. Meanwhile, the folks on the near side are wrapping short ropes around their pelvises to make rappelling harnesses, which, when done correctly, squeeze the genitals and the buttocks and feel like the mother-of-all-wedgies. These little devices of self-torture are called "Swiss seats," and they're a staple of the Army's Special Forces and Air Assault troops. The problem is, every different command has its own version of the Swiss seat. Some loop here and knot there; others do it slightly differently. The Gamecock Rangers have been tying their seats to the Air Assault standard, that used by the 101st Airborne Division at Fort Campbell. Unknown to them, Fort Jackson has been using its own version of the Swiss seat. So when the Gamecocks complete their seats and turn to show the grader, he dings them all and makes them try again.

The clock's ticking.

Finally their seats are good to go. The cadets on the near side line up on the free end of the rope. One dons thick leather gloves, lifts the rope high against the near-side post, and yells, "Pull!"

And like a team of lumberjacks at a drunken tug-o'-war, the near-siders haul on that rope for all they're worth, pulling it taut between the two posts and burning blisters into the hands of the cadet holding the rope high on the near post, in this case Ranger Daddy Courtwright. Ignoring the pain, the tension man, as Courtwright's called, grabs a little slack and wraps the rope tight around the near post. Meanwhile, Griggs joins him, quickly tying a knot to maintain the tension.

Immediately the near-siders line up where the rope meets the post. With their D-rings (metal loops with spring-loaded gates) protruding from their Swiss seats like robotic penises, they use each other as stepping stools and hook their rings to the rope. Then with a violent shove from their comrades, they haul ass down the rope and across the obstacle, pulling hand over hand until they reach the opposite post, where Fauth helps them unhook.

So it goes, one cadet at a time, until only one cadet's left on the far side. He unties the knot, gathers up the rope, and follows in Fauth's footsteps through the obstacle, ending up a muddy mess among his blistered, panting peers. When everyone's across, the grader checks the time.

A little over two minutes. Were it not for the penalties imposed by the bad Swiss seats, it'd be a competitive time.

Damn. A missed opportunity. But all's not lost.

Grenade assault goes just fine, as far as Griggs can tell. Only four cadets are required to participate, so she and the bulk of the team find a quiet spot and snooze, resting up for the short road march to the fourth event.

So far so good.

Next is the obstacle course, in which cadets slide on their backs under a web of barbed wire, scale a cargo net, cross a log, climb a hill, jump into and out of a ditch, hop over a series of metal bars, then sprint to the end. One cadet sits out. This year the lone man out is sophomore Joe Heron, whose short legs make it difficult (and potentially extremely painful) to clear the bars near the end of the course. Everyone else competes, all at the same time, negotiating each obstacle one person at a time until everybody's finished. Then the whole team moves on to the next obstacle. Things are going great until somebody gets a little too excited on the monkey bars and, with their final leap, lands atop Ranger Daddy, injuring his leg, eliminating the team's leader and strongest competitor, and dooming the Gamecocks to damn near last place, all in one ridiculous fell swoop.

Sergeant Blaylock calls Makinde at home and begs him to drive to Fort Jackson and take Courtwright's place. And, God bless him, he gamely agrees. But Makinde hasn't trained since last year and, more important, he's just not part of the team anymore.

The Gamecocks never recover from that fateful leap over the monkey bars. They slouch through weapon assembly, map reading, and the commander's event, a bizarre second obstacle course that the entire team must navigate while hauling a massive sandbag weighing several hundred pounds. Fauth and Griggs are buddies on the land nav courses, and here they excel, hitting all of their points in quick order. But it's too little too late, and the Gamecocks limp into second-to-last place.

Guess who wins? Again.

Everyone's pretty disappointed. The colonel, for his part, is furious. How dare his Rangers embarrass him like that? In front of all those other cadets and cadre no less! He's got a mind to make Ranger Challenge mandatory next year, field three or four teams and train every day whether everyone likes it or not.

Over the course of the semester he cools off. Somewhat. But then he decides the Gamecock Battalion needs an intramural basketball team. The colonel reasons that it's good exercise and it'll help morale. But even Griggs, just a freshman, could tell him how well *that*'s going to work out. Through a combination of cajoling, begging, and threatening, Moring manages to get nine cadets in uniforms and on the court for the first game of the season.

It's been a long time since Moring last coached a team, back in his former career as a high school teacher. These days his daughter's a college basketball player, and it's only whetted his appetite and raised his expectations. You can see in poor Moring's eyes desperate dreams of intramural basketball glory.

But it's not to be.

The cadets can put together a pretty good ambush. They can shoot—rifles, that is. They can march. But they can't pass a basketball to save their lives. They can't dribble. They can't shoot baskets. Their endurance, on the other hand, is excellent.

Too bad endurance doesn't score points. The cadets' first game is a solid defeat. So is their second. And so on. The colonel's dreams die fast. You can practically see his expectations tumble.

And when Ranger Challenge reconvenes in 2004, there are plenty of volunteers, but only one team. Noticeably absent is Kim Griggs, who has decided that passing eight classes is just enough challenge for her.

Besides, she's had a rough summer, involving not a little bit of failure, so maybe she's had just about all she can stand.

Capt. Alan Wilson poses with Iraqi children during a civil-affairs
mission in northern Iraq, 2004. Photo courtesy of Alan Wilson

Cadet Anderson scales the rope obstacle at Fort Jackson in September 2004.
Photo by the author

Cadet Fauth demonstrates a proper rappel for Gamecock Battalion cadets at Fort Jackson, September 2004. Photo by the author

Cadet Fauth supervises MSIs and 'IIs at Fort Jackson, September 2004. Photo by the author

Gamecock Battalion MSIs and 'IIs march in formation at Fort Jackson, September 2004. Photo by the author

LEFT: Gamecock Battalion cadets on patrol at Fort Jackson during their fall 2004 FTX. Photo courtesy of Maj. Terry Truett

BELOW: Gamecock cadets on patrol, fall 2004. Photo courtesy of Maj. Terry Truett.

Sergeant Blaylock checks out Griggs's Swiss seat before she rappels at Fort Jackson, September 2004. Photo by the author

Cadet Kim Griggs vanquishes the rope bridge at Fort Jackson, September 2004. Photo by the author

Capt. Kim Hampton, the first woman from South Carolina to die in Iraq (in January 2004), seen in her Kiowa helicopter in Iraq in 2003. Photo courtesy of the U.S. Army

The author in an Army Blackhawk en route to Iraq in January 2005.

LEFT: Capt. Jon Alexander, commander of the S.C. National Guard's 1052nd Transportation Company, seen in front of his unit's headquarters in Iraq in January 2005. Photo by the author

Flatbeds from the 1052nd line up for a convoy at Camp Anaconda, Iraq, in January 2005. Photo by the author

The South Carolina state flag flies over the 1052nd's headquarters in Iraq in January 2005. Photo by the author

Airborne 7

It's an orange night over the University of South Carolina in the summer of 2001. McLean knows these nights well: low clouds reflect the lights of the nearby downtown and cast a strange glow over the entire city. He guesses the altitude of the clouds at around two thousand feet and marvels that in three weeks, he'll jump from a perfectly good airplane at nearly the same height.

McLean spends a few more minutes skygazing, then heads back to his dorm and checks his orders one more time before turning in:

MCLEAN, WILMER, CDT
REPORT TO: HHC, 501st PIR, FORT BENNING, GA

The 501st Parachute Infantry Regiment, a unit everyone in the Army recognizes by name. Now the Airborne School training regiment, the 501st was born in 1942 by expanding the legendary test platoon that pioneered the Army's parachuting technology and techniques. Its first commander was an insane former boxer, Howard Johnson, nicknamed "Jumpy" because he loved to leap out of airplanes at high altitude—this when parachuting was in its infancy: experimental at best, damn near suicidal at worst. In 2004 even an acrophobic soldier can grit his way through Airborne, such is the rigor and science of its training. But in 1942 only people who loved hurling themselves out of rickety airplanes with a little bit of nylon tied to their backs even volunteered for Airborne training, much less made it through. Jumpy's somewhat-mad, danger-loving personality survives to this day as the ethos of the entire U.S. Army Airborne force, which includes the famed 82nd Airborne Division—fifteen-thousand strong—a separate Airborne regiment based in Italy, and a few odds and ends, including the Ranger Regiment and the seven Special Forces groups.

In 1944, after two years of training, training, training, the 501st shipped to England and joined the 101st Airborne Division, which in those days was a parachute unit but later would ditch its nylon for steel and rotors to become the Army's only helicopter-borne Air Assault division. From England, the 501st dropped into Normandy to prepare the battlefield for seaborne forces due to land on June 6.

It was a glorious fiasco. Planes scattered. Parachutists landed in tiny groups far from their objectives. For days, lost and underequipped paratroopers terrorized German-held Normandy in ad hoc units, performing improvised raids and ambushes. Almost one thousand of the regiment's two thousand men were killed, wounded, or captured. But the survivors barely slowed down. Reequipped and reinforced, only months later they dropped into Holland, where almost seven hundred, including Jumpy Johnson, became casualties. By Christmas the 501st was holed up in Bastogne, defending this key road juncture from German armored divisions with little more than their resolve and a few bazookas. Six hundred more paratroopers were lost, and the 501st secured its place in history as the kind of unit that's honored to do so much dying.

The mere thought of even temporary assignment to the 501st is enough to make McLean feel very proud and very small.

He tosses and turns in bed for several minutes and realizes that he's too nervous to sleep. So he passes the time packing and repacking his duffel bag, laying out each item and checking it against the list. Six uniforms? Twenty T-shirts? It's only a three-week course, and laundry facilities are available, so why does he need so much clothing? There's something they're not telling him.

He can repack only so many times. It's 3:00 A.M. when he locks his duffel for the last time and collapses in bed. He wills away the lists, itineraries, and contradictory advice of a dozen cadets and cadre. "Don't volunteer for anything," said the cadet battalion commander. "Volunteer for everything," said a cadet who got his wings last year.

It's too late to worry now, and it's too late to back out.

In a little more than five hours he's on a flight to Columbus, home of Fort Benning and the U.S. Army Airborne School.

There are a dozen soldiers on the plane with him, judging by all the uniforms. McLean strains to see their shoulder patches and badges. From these little pieces of cloth, he can tell a lot about the wearer. On their left shoulders, every soldier wears the emblem of their parent division. A big red "1" represents the 1st Infantry Division, the poor bastards who bought Omaha Beach in blood fifty-seven years ago. A checkerboard represents the 3rd Infantry Division, successors to the 24th Infantry Division, which charged the length of Kuwait in only one hundred hours in 1991.

Soldiers know all the war stories. They take pride in them. They draw inspiration from them. While there are only a handful of soldiers in the 3rd ID who were in the 24th ID for its heroic race to Iraq, every one of the unit's fifteen thousand soldiers *feels* as if he were there. It's called esprit de corps, and even civilians feel it sometimes. Who doesn't get a little excited when they see the screaming eagle patch of the 101st Airborne Division, the unit that held the line when the rest of the Army turned tail at the Battle of the Bulge?

Of course no one on the plane's wearing a 101st patch. Or, for that matter, the "All-American" patch of the 82nd Airborne. After all, if you're wearing either of those patches, you've probably already been to Airborne or Air Assault, the equivalent school for the 101st's helicopter-borne troops.

Most of the patches McLean sees, he doesn't recognize. He guesses they represent training units. Which figures. Fort Benning *is* the first stop for a lot of new recruits and young officers—and cadets, too, it seems. McLean recognizes at least one other cadet on the plane by virtue of his lame-ass ROTC shoulder patch, a shield with quadrants containing a lamp and an ancient Greek helmet, representing knowledge and warfare respectively. ROTC's patch inspires a lot of ridicule from regular soldiers. It doesn't help that most ROTC units also wear patches on their right shoulders representing their schools. In the real Army, the right shoulder is reserved for combat patches. When a soldier sees combat, he is authorized to wear on his right shoulder the patch of the unit he was with at the time. For most of the '80s and '90s, right shoulder patches were relatively rare. The Gulf War resulted in a couple hundred thousand new combat patches, but over time many of those vets left the Army. In 2001 the combat patch again is relatively rare. But in only a couple years, the situation will change dramatically. By late 2004 soldiers with bare right shoulders will be the exception to the rule.

Unsurprisingly, most of the soldiers on McLean's plane have naked right shoulders. In fact their entire uniforms are rather bare. Over the course of a twenty-year career, soldiers tend to accumulate a lot of patches: Airborne wings, Air Assault wings, scuba patches, sapper patches, a drill sergeant's massive circular badge. A soldier's uniform is only uniform in the most general sense of the word. Few wear the same combination of patches, badges and wings. Every soldier's uniform is like a pressed, camouflaged, wearable resume.

For his part, McLean has prudently removed his right shoulder patch, a matter of decorum when venturing off campus. So his resume is pretty sparse. But Lord willing that will change in three weeks when he earns the right to sew on brand-new Airborne wings.

But first he's got to get past the pissed-off sergeant at the arrival gate. The sergeant is dividing the arriving soldiers into groups for transport to Fort Benning. He has the weary air of a man who has spent too many hours processing anonymous faces into an anonymous system. He seems to look *through* soldiers instead of *at* them as he manhandles them into their groups.

There are dozens of soldiers: privates, corporals, a few NCOs, and a handful of cadets—one of whom, McLean notes, is in civilian clothes ("civvies"), and another of whom is still wearing his school patch on his right shoulder.

The surly sergeant notes the patch, too. He parts the crowd and stares down one of the unwitting cadets. "Who the hell are you?"

"Cadet Johnson, Sergeant."

The other soldiers snicker and roll their eyes. The sergeant steps closer, craning to come nose to nose with Johnson. "You seen combat, Cadet?"

Johnson can't help but smile. "Um, no, Sergeant."

The NCO is not amused. "I have," he says. He taps his right shoulder with his left thumb. McLean recognizes the patch of the 2nd Armored Cavalry Regiment. This man massacred Iraqi soldiers in the Kuwaiti desert.

The sergeant continues. "I don't know what goes on at . . . ," he squints to read Johnson's shoulder patch, "wherever. But you in the *real* Army, now, Cadet. And this shit don't fly." He grabs the corner of Johnson's school patch and rips it off in one motion, taking a significant chunk of uniform with it. The crowd's snickers turn to muffled laughter. The sergeant turns his attention to the cadet in civvies. "What the fuck is this?"

The cadet drops his duffel bag and comes to parade rest, his eyes fixed on a point somewhere over the NCO's right shoulder. "Cadet Byrd, Sergeant."

"You travelin' incognito, Cadet?"

"No, Sergeant."

"Then maybe you're Special Forces."

"No, Sergeant."

"Haircut seems like it," the sergeant says, referring to the relaxed haircut standards shared by the Army's top commandoes and lowliest cadets.

"Yes, Sergeant."

"You call that parade rest?"

"Yes, Sergeant. I mean, no, Sergeant."

"Which one, hero?"

"I . . . I don't know, Sergeant."

He looks at the bag at Byrd's feet. "I hope you got something green in that lumpy-ass duffel of yours."

"Yes, Sergeant."

"Well, hero?"

Byrd glances down and makes momentary eye contact with the belligerent NCO. The sergeant nods his head in the direction of the restrooms, and Byrd double-times across the baggage claim to the refuge of the men's room. In two minutes flat he's properly clothed and blending in nicely. McLean feels a sympathetic flush of relief. Soon, the NCO loads everyone into an un-air-conditioned van for the ride to Fort Benning. It's a ten-minute trip, but it feels like an hour.

Fort Benning is one of the busiest posts in the nation. And one of the hottest. Perhaps it's appropriate that the division to which most of the Airborne students are headed, the famed 82nd Airborne, soon will have subordinate units deployed to Iraq and Afghanistan. As they say in the Department of Defense, train as you fight. That means train hard and often regardless of the heat index.

It's barely 10:00 A.M. when McLean and his comrades arrive for in-processing, and it's already close to ninety degrees. He's coated in sweat five minutes after stepping off the van. And it only gets worse. There are so many arriving students that McLean and his group are ordered to stand in formation and wait. Soon he's drenched. Now he realizes why his packing list required twenty T-shirts. He'll easily sweat through three or four per day. Too bad he can't get to them now. He's too busy waiting.

Hurry up and wait. It's a favorite saying of Army personnel. Nothing happens in the U.S. Army without documentation in triplicate. And in an organization that considers the 286 computer the cutting edge of technology, documentation can take a while. Fortunately, waiting is the one useful military skill the university has taught him. McLean just does what he always did while waiting in line for registration: he relaxes his body, closes his eyes, and loses himself in memories and dreams.

He remembers his first day at the university, two years ago. He remembers the fear, the excitement, and, above all, the sense of awe at the overwhelming size and complexity of the institutions and events all around him. He remembers his induction into ROTC—the bustle, the paperwork, the parade of names and faces and titles and acronyms: DOD, LBE, BDU. Not only did he face the same challenges as his non-ROTC classmates—homework, bills, homesickness —he also had to adapt to a military culture and learn its language. It was terrifying. But the fear was mixed with excitement about all the things he would learn and what he might become at the end of it all.

But as active as his freshman imagination was, he never dreamed that in two years, he'd travel hundreds of miles to the busiest base in the Army and learn to jump out of airplanes.

"Group, attention!"

McLean snaps to attention and opens his eyes to see a distracted-looking sergeant holding a clipboard. "Listen up, legs. You will now in-process. When you are done, you will go to your company for briefing and billeting. Any questions?" He barely pauses. "Good. Welcome to Airborne School, you miserable dirt darts."

The next seventy-two hours is a slow-motion blur. He's amazed at how much time he can spend doing so little, and how tired he can be without knowing exactly what he's accomplished. It takes two days to knock out all the administrative details. By day three, McLean is exhausted—just in time to start training.

He quickly learns the lingo:

Black Hat: an experienced Airborne School trainer

Sergeant Airborne: what Airborne students call their instructors

Leg: any soldier who's not Airborne-qualified; variations include "lego,"
    "legola," "legosaur," "legobot," and "Doctor Legenstein"

Cherry: a new parachutist with only the five qualifying jumps under his belt

Dirt dart: an Airborne soldier with a malfunctioning parachute

Sky shark: an Airborne soldier who is a threat to other soldiers in the air

And he learns what it takes to survive. Blending in is an important skill, and he wonders if the cadet who recommended that he volunteer for everything was pulling a prank on him—or worse, trying to set him up for failure. McLean reminds himself to have a little chat with the individual once he gets back to USC.

If he gets back. In the closed environment of Airborne School, the rumors, myths, lies, and legends spread fast: The last cycle lost two jumpers in a freak static line accident. An observer from the German Bundeswehr got sucked out of the jump door and impaled on a fence post. The beetles in the sawdust pit are poisonous.

As bad as these rumors are, there's one that's far worse, and far more likely: the Black Hats try to fail cadets. McLean isn't sure how true it is. So far, the Black Hats seem to treat everyone the same—that is, badly. Barracks inspections are strict, contraband such as food brings swift retribution, and all breaches of discipline are punished—first with late-night guard duty, then with gleeful dismissal from the school.

For cadets, dismissal isn't so bad, really. They pack up, go home, and maybe get yelled at by their cadre. But for the enlisted soldiers, the consequences are truly grave. "They send you straight to Korea," one soldier tells McLean. He's not sure if it's true. But it's no lie that for an enlisted man to fail Airborne School is a permanent blight on his record, and he won't get another chance. Unlike cadets, who can get an Airborne slot simply by asking, enlisted men wait for months or years for a shot at earning their wings. For the average private, Airborne School is an important rite of passage. For cadets it's a glorified summer camp. McLean can feel the resentment radiating from his enlisted peers. It certainly doesn't make Airborne School any easier.

Training is tough. Again, McLean feels deceived by fellow cadets back home who dismissed Airborne as a cakewalk. "Just hang around," one cadet said. "Airborne's a three-week exercise in patience."

That much is true. But the challenge is real. There's PT every morning, marching under the hot sun, and long hours standing in constricting parachute harnesses. And then there's the mental challenge: this is no ROTC weekend getaway with rubber weapons and bathroom breaks. The schedule is packed, albeit with a lot of scheduled waiting around, and expectations are high. McLean watches a steady stream of dropouts from injuries, heat exhaustion, or failure to perform to standard. McLean manages, but barely.

Airborne School is divided into three phases of one week apiece. Ground week introduces students to the fundamentals of military parachuting: the equipment, the terminology, the ethos and—most important—the parachute landing fall, or PLF. They spend hours practicing falling in a controlled manner, striking five points of contact in the right order: heels, knees, thighs, butt, and back. The PLF distributes the force of a parachutist's landing in such a way that no single bone bears all the weight. Jumpers who screw up their PLFs are lucky to limp off the drop zone. Others leave on stretchers. A dozen of McLean's classmates are kicked out after repeatedly failing to demonstrate a proper PLF. Luckily he masters it fairly quickly and moves on to week two: tower week, the last obstacle before jump week.

It's in week two that McLean discovers something he never knew about himself: he's terrified of heights. The heart of tower week is several days of training from the forty-foot tower, essentially a wooden platform atop a flight of steps. The platform is connected to the ground by way of a one-hundred-foot cable. Students in their painful harnesses climb the steps and wait in line to hook up and slide down the cable to a sandy mound, where they will demonstrate a proper PLF. McLean realizes, as he ascends, that the feeling welling up in his stomach isn't indigestion from the fatty chow. For the first time in his life he literally *tastes* fear—irrational, debilitating fear. And it tastes like acid.

A Black Hat stops him halfway up the tower. "You look pale, Legosaur. What's your malfunction?"

McLean swallows a mouthful of bile. "Feel sick, Sergeant Airborne."

"That ain't sick, leg. That's scared. You know why it's a forty-foot tower?"

"No, Sergeant Airborne."

The Black Hat grins. "'Cause fear starts at forty feet. It's a test, Lego."

So he stands at the open maw of empty space beyond the edge of the tower with his harness hooked to the cable and a line of impatient soldiers stacking up behind him. He knows it's only forty feet, but it seems like a thousand. And now he understands why. Fear of heights is an on/off switch flipped at forty feet. The flightless animal in his reptile brain makes no distinction between forty feet and forty thousand. Both mean death if he falls.

Suddenly McLean regrets volunteering for Airborne School. Who does he think he is? He's a college junior and a damned ROTC cadet. Sure, ROTC is fun, especially when they play team sports for PT. But he didn't count on this: facing death at forty feet. This shit is for real.

McLean is about to turn around and beg the Black Hat to unhook him and send him home when the company first sergeant bellows from below, "What's the hold-up, Sergeant?"

"No hold-up, First Sergeant," the Black Hat says.

Before he can protest, McLean feels himself lifted off the platform. His feet are kicking open air and his stomach is performing backflips. A chorus of his peers pipes up from the ground and the tower in a spontaneous cry of "Airborne!" and McLean sails screaming through space. Five seconds later, his feet execute a perfect PLF without being told, and before he knows it, a couple of enlisted men pick him off the ground and dust him off. They steady him, unhook his harness from the cable, and push him back towards the tower.

There are two more tower jumps to go. Then he's on to jump week and the real thing. He smiles despite the raging ocean of acid in his stomach and the weakness in his legs. For the first time in his brief military career, McLean feels like a soldier.

Then it's jump week, the Holy Grail of Airborne School. Five jumps are required to graduate. It's a favorite bit of trivia among eager legs that injuries before the fifth jump are disqualifying, but injuries incurred *during* the jump *aren't*. A soldier earns his wings the moment he leaves the plane for the fifth time. He can even *die* on the fifth jump and still graduate.

Students going into jump week know by now how dangerous military parachuting is. They've heard all the stories. There's the kid who lost the digits on his right hand when he accidentally deployed his reserve parachute and the suspension lines wrapped around his fingers. There's the soldier who got caught up on the plane and dragged through the air for several miles. There are stories of faulty parachutes, midair collisions and entanglements, concussions and shattered bones upon landing, and so on. And the students know the statistics: 10 percent of soldiers in any military jump will be injured in some way. But no one believes it will happen to him.

The preparation is intense. Wake at 4:00 A.M., eat a quick breakfast, and head straight to the equipment shed on the other side of post to don harnesses and parachutes. And then there are hours of inspections. The Black Hats' professionalism has never been more evident. Suddenly the Black Hats are more than sadistic jokers; now they're the guys who will keep you alive.

Every student's harness is inspected several times: a Black Hat checks every knot, loop, and fold in the complicated system of straps and buckles that is the T-10 parachute harness. But even in the dead-serious business of harness inspection, the Black Hats find room for their twisted collective sense of humor. McLean is sitting on the bench awaiting his next inspection when he hears a sergeant exclaim, "I'll be damned!"

McLean looks up to see a Black Hat with his hands on his hips, shaking his head as a wide-eyed cadet struggles to remain upright under the weight of his main chute, reserve chute, and harness. Something's not right, something about the way the cadet's harness hangs low around his hips.

The sergeant gestures to nearby Black Hats. "Hey, check this out," he says. The Black Hats form a critical circle around the poor cadet, all attention on his peculiar drooping harness. "You ever seen anything like it?" the first Black Hat asks the others. They shake their heads. "Weirdest thing I ever seen," one says, tugging at the harness as the cadet's eyes grow even wider and sweat pours down his face, despite the powerful air-conditioning. "What went wrong?"

"Nothing's wrong," the first Black Hat says. "It's just him." He slaps the cadet's shoulders. "He's shaped weird."

The cadet swallows audibly.

The Black Hats stand around rubbing their chins and making curious asides to each other for several minutes before one says, "Hope it holds," and returns to his work. The other Black Hats shrug and go back to their inspections one at a time until only the original sergeant remains. He finishes the cadet's inspection with a tug on the harness. "Congratulations, Cadet," he says. "You're going to make history."

McLean is confident that he has mastered his fear of heights. Fear starts at forty feet, and he's already conquered forty. But he realizes soon after boarding the C-130 Hercules cargo plane that he also gets motion sick. The C-130 is older than anyone on board, including the Air Force pilots. It rattles and shakes like an overloaded washing machine even while on the ground. After five minutes in the cavelike, metal hold, McLean is pale, clammy, and struggling to keep from vomiting his breakfast. Despite his state, he can't help but laugh when a fellow student falls asleep in the seat next to him.

He knows he's not going to die. But knowing and believing are two different things. And as the ramp closes and the aircraft begins to taxi, McLean's life literally flashes before his eyes. He sees a parade of memories and images and even premonitions. He sees himself as a child, playing war in the woods behind his house. He sees himself, a bit older, wearing a Boy Scout uniform with a brand-new service badge. And there he is at high school graduation, clutching a framed award from the Army recognizing him as the privileged recipient of a four-year ROTC scholarship. And now he sees himself in the near future wearing a lieutenant's bars and shiny, silver wings. Despite the sickness and the dread of gravity and death, there is a tiny germ of pride and courage. So help him God, he will make it through. Even if he pisses himself or vomits on the Black Hat at the jump door, he will make it through.

The Hercules takes flight. Minutes later, before McLean has time to gather his scattered emotions into any kind of unified terror, the Black Hat standing at the rear of the hold throws open the jump door and leans into the open air to scan the drop zone. He turns to the seated jumpers and raises one finger. A call is passed down the line: "One minute!"

McLean is no longer thinking. Somewhere in the estranged front of his brain, he realizes that his training has taken over. And for a Zen moment, his fear dissipates. He's a parachutist, just one of hundreds in the air at this moment. He's been trained by the finest body of professionals in the world. He's carried aloft by fifty years of Airborne tradition and the gracious support of the U.S. Air Force. He's a soldier in the mightiest army in the history of the world. What can possibly go wrong?

The warnings come quickly, then the commands.

"Stand up!" McLean and his stick of fifteen other jumpers stand and press together.

"Hook up!" They hook yellow lines to a cable running along the ceiling of the aircraft.

"Equipment check!" Each jumper checks the parachute of the jumper in front of him.

Seconds later the red light next to the jump door turns green, and the Black Hat yells, "Go!"

The stick of jumpers feeds out the door one at a time.

Now McLean is falling through blinding white space. He feels nothing. He thinks nothing. He doesn't comprehend the perfect functioning of his training and equipment.

As he leaves the aircraft, he tucks his arms and head into his chest to avoid flailing and spinning. His feet and knees remain tightly pressed together. His yellow static line, attached to the cable inside the aircraft, goes taut and yanks McLean's parachute from its pack. The canopy deploys in a flawless explosion of fabric. McLean is jerked, yanked, and jarred, and then there is stillness and the gentle rush of wind in his ears. His free fall has become a controlled descent.

His mouth falls open. He sees the drop zone like a miniature landscape, 1,200 feet below. There are parachutes like giant wildflowers everywhere. The wind is calm, the sunshine warm and pleasant.

McLean is flying.

He hears himself screaming at the top of his lungs: "Airborne!"

One down, four to go. No problem. As he descends, McLean experiences a new sensation. Even if he breaks a leg on the drop zone or collides with another jumper and burns in like a dirt dart from hell, even if he loses his scholarship, fails an exam, or gets rejected by a girl, nothing can hurt him ever again.

He's invulnerable.

He's immortal.

He's a soldier.

High and Right 8

It's hard not to feel confident when you're young. And when you're young and fit, with a fresh high-and-tight haircut and a brand-new pair of Airborne wings, like Wil McLean is, that confidence runs especially high.

It's a typical college morning. At 9:00 the working world is sitting at its cubicle, refilling on coffee, or stuck in rush hour traffic. But on the campus of the University of South Carolina, half the student body is sound asleep, and some of them went to bed only hours earlier. Life at college starts a few hours later than it does elsewhere.

But tell that to McLean, Coe, Fauth, and the rest of the Gamecock Battalion. This morning, they awoke at 5:30 for a 6:00 formation, beating all but the earliest-rising businessfolk. Identically dressed in gray physical-fitness uniforms with "ARMY" in big black letters across their chests, lined up in ranks on the dew-soaked grass of a city park adjacent to campus, sounding off at the command of their leaders, the Gamecock Battalion looks like the loudest and most disciplined army of ghosts ever to grace the living world.

Commands echo off fog-shrouded trees and startle squirrels and slumbering birds. In nearby dorms and apartments, dozing undergrads rouse slightly at the sound, maybe mutter a profanity or two under their breaths, then snuggle deeper into the beds, futons, or couches. Outside they hear gruff voices yell:

"Fall in!"

"Attention!"

"Dress right, dress!"

The battalion is divided into platoons. Each platoon is led by a cadet platoon leader and a cadet platoon sergeant. The platoon leader takes attendance, while the platoon sergeant works the formation. If someone's missing, phone calls are made. If phone calls don't work, someone may run to the sleepyhead's dorm and drag their sorry ass out of bed.

Nobody misses PT.

Just ask McLean. Last year, just once, he overslept. Before he knew it, he'd been summoned to Lieutenant Colonel Buchanan's office and told to stand at attention. In that position, you're not supposed to make eye contact with your superior, just stare over his shoulder at some point on the wall. That has the effect of disabling your natural instinct to track danger, making you feel vulnerable. It also elevates your superior by making you unworthy of even looking at him.

Buchanan's speech was short and it boiled down to this: It's not about missing PT. McLean is in good shape and everyone knows it; he doesn't need the exercise. But he *does* need to work on his leadership skills, and that's what PT's really all about. "How can you expect your soldiers to come to PT, if you don't," said Buchanan. He repeated his favorite admonition, one McLean would quote for years to come. "You've got to be in the right place, at the right time, in the right uniform."

The rest is just details.

Back on that foggy field, with early commuters whizzing by in their compact cars and SUVs, soon everyone is accounted for. Those who are absent will be gracing the colonel's office after class.

The platoon sergeants order their platoons to fall out. Everybody grabs a buddy and a piece of real estate. Sergeant Blaylock strides into the center of the field full of cadets and opens up his windpipes. He uses his sergeant voice.

"The next exercise is the push-up!"

Here and there a few cadets really feeling the adrenaline echo, "The push-up!"

With an NCO calling out the pace like a metronome or the world's ugliest conductor, one cadet in each buddy-team goes up and down with his feet planted, his back straight, and his hands flat on the ground, shoulder-length apart. His buddy keeps a fist, with the thumb raised, under his chest to make sure he goes down far enough. During regular physical-fitness tests, which everyone in the Army is required to pass, graders will count out the number of successful push-ups. Fail to touch that thumb and the grader will repeat the last number.

"Forty-nine. Forty-nine. Forty-nine. Lower. Lower!"

Some cadets have nightmares about that thumb and that number, repeated over and over until muscles fail and Army careers come crashing down onto the cold, wet grass of some bleak field early, early in the morning.

McLean is good at PT. Coe's not bad. But the real PT hero of the Gamecock Battalion is Makinde. He does push-ups like he's spring loaded. His sit-ups look effortless. He doesn't run the physical fitness test's two-mile course; he sprints it.

There's room for heroics when it comes to PT. You may start out in formation; you end in formation, too. But in between there's a chance to stand out, to do 100 push-ups, 150 sit-ups, and outrun the pack. Lest you get carried away, from time to time the Gamecock Battalion does formation runs.

PT studs hate formation runs because they're not fast or long enough. PT wimps hate them because they're too fast and too long—and if you fall out, throw up, or faint, everyone sees it. But none of its detractors can deny it: formation runs are damn impressive.

Imagine a hundred cadets and their trainers running side by side in several rows with their battalion banner whipping in the wind up front. Alongside runs a cadet or a sergeant whose job it is to call out cadence. The caller sings and the choir of bobbing heads responds:

CALLER:
Put a hundred ragheads up against the wall
Make a $5 bet I can kill them all
Sound off
Sound off
Sound off

FORMATION:
Put a hundred ragheads up against the wall
Make a $5 bet I can kill them all
One, two
three, four
One, two, three, four, one, two, three, four

There are hundreds of cadences in circulation in the U.S. Army, some of them deliciously racist and sexist, others like time capsules of bygone eras, such as the cadence about a Viet Cong mortar attack on a barracks full of lazy soldiers and one hard-assed sergeant. Some particularly chauvinistic cadences reflect the long-gone, all-male Army:

Jesse James said before he died
There were just three things he would like to ride
Bicycle, tricycle, automobile
The general's daughter on a Ferris wheel

That particular cadence is usually banned in ROTC—and so are any with vulgar language or sexual references. The prohibitions encourage cadets to get creative.

Oldies make good cadences:

CALLER:
CALLER:

There she was, just a-walking down the street

FORMATION:

Singing doo wah diddy diddy dum diddy doo

So do rhymes that couch the vulgarities in vague language, like this one—
ostensibly about a sailor and his rope:

> The first mate, the first mate
> His rope, it was a big one
> He wrapped it twice around the mast
> And used the rest for riggin'

Anyone with a large repertoire of cadences and a decent singing voice is
treasured. A caller with rhythm and volume helps the formation stay in step
and keep pace. When a caller's on and the formation's really digging it, a run
like this can be a bona fide musical event: feet stomping rhythm, caller singing
loud and clear, the formation responding with the deep bark of a hundred
voices in unison. There's no better demonstration of what it looks, sounds, and
feels like to belong to a military unit.

When the mood's right, formation runs can evoke a kind of euphoria, especially for cadets high on their growing strength, confidence, and competence.
Fresh from Airborne School, silver wings gleaming on the uniform jacket in
his closet, that feeling of flight still fresh in his mind, McLean is really feeling
this run. He sings louder and louder. He pounds the pavement harder and
harder in rhythm with the song. Even his heart beats in time. And then the
caller bridges to a new cadence, a personal favorite of many cadets.

The Airborne cadence. It goes like this:

> C-130 rolling down the strip
> Airborne Daddy gonna take a little trip
> Mission top-secret, destination unknown
> Don't even know if he's ever coming home
> Stand up, hook up, shuffle to the door
> Jump right out and count to four
> If my chute don't open wide
> I got another right by my side
> If that one should fail me, too
> Look out below I'm coming through
> If I die on the ol' drop zone
> Box me up and ship me home
> Pin my medals upon my chest

Tell my momma I done my best
Airborne
Ranger

With his own five Airborne jumps still fresh in his adrenal glands, McLean gets a little carried away, and so do the cadets around him. It spreads. Soon the entire formation is buzzing with energy and sounding off loud enough to make dogs howl and birds take flight.

What Webster's calls esprit de corps the Army calls hooah. Dozens of sleepy undergrads awoken by the clamor call it rude. The formation winds through the center of campus and past the two-hundred-year-old theater that once served as a Confederate hospital and is said to be haunted by the ghosts of wounded soldiers. Past the Caroliniana Library with its collections of letters penned by soldiers in a dozen wars. Past sagging, late-nineteenth-century Legare College. The collective voice of cadets and cadre echoes back and forth across the lawn, as pissed-off upperclassmen lift their windows and yell, "Shut up!" To campus residents regularly awoken by formation runs, ROTC is a joke. Aside from some stupid civil wars in places nobody ever worried about like Chechnya and Afghanistan and the occasional bombing of an African embassy or a Navy destroyer, the world's at peace, and that's not going to change. The cold war's over, people. All these students running around in uniform singing about lining ragheads up against walls are training for wars that'll never happen. They're an anachronism. On top of that, they're plain annoying.

It's September 2001, dude. War's out of style.

TWO

War in the Blood 9

Nobody wants to admit it, but South Carolina's got a love affair with violence. All that southern hospitality, all those pastel colors, fatty foods, and that public obsession with God and family—they're a veneer on an ugly reality. In 2001 South Carolina is ranked sixth in the nation in violent crime and first in domestic violence, according to the FBI. Myrtle Beach has one of the highest crime rates of all American cities, and Columbia's pretty high on the list, too, with a murder rate of 12 per 100,000 in 2003, versus New York City's 7.

It's not a new phenomenon. Misery has always had a home in South Carolina, never more so than in 1865, when the Union Army slashed and burned its way to the city and occupied the campus of South Carolina College. Massive fires swept Columbia in the immediate aftermath of the Union occupation. To this day, historians are divided on whether it was coincidence or not, whether during the occupation some old lady's cow happened to kick over a lantern, or a cooking fire just got tragically out of control—or if torch-wielding Union soldiers, bitter from years of bloodshed, exacted a little revenge on the first state to secede.

War and reconstruction devastated South Carolina. Its young men were dead or disabled. Its slaves were free. Its crops were burned and its infrastructure destroyed. For the next century, South Carolina would be poor, underdeveloped, and underpopulated. The result in 2004? An infant mortality rate of 950 per 100,000, versus 720 nationally. In South Carolina, 76 percent have high school diplomas, versus 80 percent nationally. Not to mention high crime, outdated infrastructure, reactionary politics, low wages, and depressed real estate values.

But it's not all misery. Some have benefited from South Carolina's relative backwardness, among them big organizations in need of cheap land and labor. For instance, the federal government, in the form of first the War Department and later the Department of Defense. After unrestricted submarine warfare drew the United States into World War I, South Carolina was the perfect place to build some of the brand-new camps necessary to expand the tiny U.S. Army into a force capable of making a difference in Europe. The Army went shopping for land near the state capital, and boy did it ever get a deal. Caught up in a patriotic thrall and eager for the jobs a new camp would create, the city of Columbia donated several thousand acres to the War Department. Camp Jackson, later Fort Jackson, sprang up nearly overnight.

It has grown steadily ever since. In 2004 it's one of the biggest training posts in the Army, processing fifty thousand soldiers every year.

Fort Jackson's not alone. Nearby in Sumter County are two Air Force bases. Charleston is home to sprawling Navy facilities and another Air Force base. The Marine Corps trains half of its recruits at Parris Island and flies fighter jets out of an air station in Beaufort. In all, there are 75,000 military personnel in South Carolina, as well as nearly half a million veterans, military retirees, and dependents. The military pumps $7 billion annually into the state's economy.

So it's no surprise that both the Senate and House Armed Services Committees count prominent members from South Carolina. War is big business here.

But it's more than that. War is part of the state's culture and of the culture of the entire region. Around half of the military hails from the South. By November 2004, thirty South Carolinians had died in Iraq and Afghanistan, the eighth highest death rate by the twenty-sixth most populous state. Meanwhile, the S.C. National Guard, the tenth biggest in the country, has deployed four thousand people to the war zone. The entire nation of Great Britain, by comparison, has fewer than ten thousand personnel deployed.

Despite the cost in blood and to the state's workforce, the wars remain as popular as ever in South Carolina. Every military victory prompts a flurry of press releases from lawmakers. Every returning company of National Guardsmen gets a parade and a barbeque. And at a time when most Americans have retired the old flags they flew after September 11, the Stars and Stripes is still everywhere in Columbia, even painted ten feet high on the side of a popular Five Points tavern.

South Carolina loves violence, especially when it's called war. No wonder the state boasts twenty-two ROTC units at its sixty-two colleges and universities, versus just 270 at all of America's three thousand schools. And they're not just numerous. ROTC units at schools such as USC, the Citadel, and Furman are widely recognized as some of the best in the country.

Best, that is, in making professional killers out of college students like Wil McLean, who after graduating heads straight to Infantry Officer Basic Course at Fort Benning. OBC is sixteen weeks of PT and FTXs, like Advanced Camp times ten and minus the suck. But to McLean, it's a cakewalk. A lot of ROTC cadets fall through the cracks, especially in things of a tactical nature. But somehow McLean turned out all right.

Or better than all right. He breezes through OBC and heads straight to a six-week mechanized infantry leader's course. Then a four-week course on the M-3A3 Bradley fighting vehicle, a sort of hollow tank for carrying around infantry. After that, it's off to Fort Hood, Texas, to await his first platoon. In the interim, he hooks up with a former sniper instructor for some informal training in shooting people in the head from one thousand yards away. And after a year of nonstop training, McLean has some perspective on his stint in ROTC.

If you do it right, ROTC is not only good preparation for the moral and emotional aspects of leadership, but for the professional and technical aspects as well. Everything McLean needed to know was there to learn: land nav, weapons assembly, basic marksmanship, squad tactics, and the all-important operations order, the OPORD, the Army's template for briefing upcoming missions.

As an MSIV, McLean delivered dozens of briefings to the cadre. While the operations he was briefing were very real—APFTs and FTXs for example—the briefings themselves were half the point. How better to learn the OPORD than to use it, week after week, in the relatively low-stress environment of ROTC, where a fucked-up OPORD may piss off the colonel and put a kink in your weekend plans, but it isn't going to get anyone killed.

More than anything else, it's his dedicated ROTC cadre that McLean credits with preparing him for the real Army. Years after both McLean and his old cadre have moved onto bigger and better things in their Army careers, he can still recite their names and cite their influences.

Major Jacobs, the very first female honor graduate of Airborne School in the whole Army, told McLean what to expect when he attended the school himself. Her most important advice: "Do what they tell you."

Master Sergeant Lesane, a former first sergeant in the 82nd Airborne and one of the most professional soldiers McLean has ever met, taught him attention to detail and drilled into his head that excuses were unacceptable in the U.S. Army.

Major Burnett listened to McLean's briefings and helped him get them into shape for the colonel—thankless duty, to be sure, but essential. Because of Burnett, McLean can write OPORDs in his sleep.

Every OPORD looks more or less the same, regardless of what event it briefs. Even if the event were, say, one of the USC cadets' frequent excursions to the local bar scene, the OPORD would still adhere to an Army-wide format, spoken by the planner like so:

> My name is Wil McLean, and I will be social chair for Thursday night.
> Take out a pen and paper and prepare to copy. Please hold all questions
> until the end.

Situation.

Enemy forces tonight include ID-checking bouncers, suspicious bartenders, members of local law enforcement, belligerent fraternity types, drunken fat chicks, and the debilitating effects of extreme quantities of alcohol. Expect the enemy to be aggressive, persistent, and reactive. The enemy is capable of spreading disease, leading to arrest, and causing embarrassing social situations, potentially resulting in dismissal from ROTC.

Friendly forces tonight include all of us and anybody we invite along. Bring your buddies. Bring your girlfriends. Bring your lame roommate, the one always sitting around apartment on a Thursday night because he's "got work to do." Higher's intent is that we stay home and study, but fuck higher. Let's get lit!

There are no attachments, unless of course we pick up some hotties looking to score. And no detachments, unless somebody gets really drunk and passes out in the bathroom or just has to catch a cab home.

Mission.

All drinkers in the Gamecock Battalion will conduct alcohol consumption from happy hour till the wee hours of the morning in the vicinity of Five Points, down thataway, probably at Delaney's to start with, in order to numb our pain and loneliness and artificially increase our self-confidence and self-esteem.

I say again! All drinkers in the Gamecock Battalion will conduct alcohol consumption in order to numb our pain and increase our self-esteem!

Execution.

It is my intent that we happy few, we band of brothers, be prepared to get shit-faced and be on time for happy hour, which starts in, oh, ten minutes.

Concept of the operation.

Tonight's drinking will be conducted in three phases.

Phase one. Drink at Delaney's until they kick us out.

Phase two. Drink somewhere else until *they* kick us out.

Phase three. Drink at my place until we *pass* out.

Task to maneuver units.

Makinde. You're driving.

Fauth. You're the token female.

Gillespie. Try to keep your pants on.

Coordinating instructions.

Timeline.

Drinking starts in seven minutes. Anybody who needs a ride, Makinde's got the hookup.

Maps and routes.

Damn it, you all know where Delaney's is. We were there last week and the week before, remember?

Safety.

Drink plenty of water and piss often. Beer before wine, everything's fine. Beer after liquor, never been sicker.

Service support.

Supply.

Everybody got their fake IDs and plenty of cash?

Transportation.

Nobody puke in Makinde's car.

Medevac.

If you *do* need to puke, do it in the bathroom. If things get real nasty, we'll call you a cab and you can puke at home.

Command and signal.

Like I said, I'm your social chair. But if shit goes down, I'm out of here. Ain't one of you worth my damn scholarship. If you can't find me, find Fauth. She's cool.

The time is now happy hour minus three minutes. Who's got questions?"

All joking aside, cadets at USC drink a lot, but no more than noncadets. Columbia, like most college towns, has more bars than churches, and despite blue laws that limited alcohol sales on Sunday and required that all liquor be served from airline bottles, selling booze to college kids is one of the city's major industries. From Thursday night through Sunday morning, you can hear bottles breaking, men hollering, car horns honking, and sirens screaming—all coming from Five Points and the USC campus. Crime peaks during drinking hours. There are fights, fake IDs, aggressive begging by the small army of homeless people drawn to the lights and the sounds, and auto break-ins on crowded lots too numerous for patrolling cops to cover.

Of course it's unfair to fault ROTC cadets when drinking is a major pastime Army-wide. Alcoholics Anonymous groups meet in chow halls at forward bases in Iraq, where—technically speaking—drinking is outlawed. But soldiers find a way, and illegal stills inevitably crop up during long deployments.

Whether alcohol consumption is like this in other countries is anybody's guess, and whether there's a connection between American soldiers' drinking and their world-famous fierceness is a matter of speculation. It may be merely coincidence that Army commanders tried to crack down on what was reportedly a serious problem with alcohol abuse at Abu Ghraib prison just weeks before the prisoner-abuse scandal broke.

How to Fail 10

Sure, the standards in the Gamecock Battalion are lax enough that drinkers get away with being drinkers. But it's not that ROTC's not hard. In fact, plenty of folks join up and drop out within weeks. They figure out just how much time is required; they get yelled at for the first time in their lives; they learn that joining the Army means surrendering your First Amendment rights; or they get their first look at a live weapon and realize that this shit's for real.

You can usually tell them, the ones who won't last. They're the ones who look queasy in formation, constantly bitch about lost sleep, and act surprised and outraged when the leadership reminds them that they've got training this weekend.

One demographic particularly prone to quit is black females. For some reason, every year a dozen or so join up, only to drop out within a week or two. Nobody's quite sure what draws them to ROTC in the first place—nobody except them, of course, but they're not talking. Maybe it's the uniforms. Maybe it's the promise of camaraderie. But it's pretty clear what changes their minds: PT. You can count on three out of four black women dropping out, which is maybe one reason why black women are underrepresented in the Army, accounting for only 3 percent of the officer corps.

On the other hand, sometimes failure strikes where least expected. After all, the Army has high standards and lots of them. From height-weight ratio to visual acuity and color blindness, criminal background to philosophical tendencies, there are a lot of little ways soldiers are expected to measure up. Moral reservations about violence are disqualifying. So are felonies and even misdemeanor drug offenses. Adultery is a no-no. So is falling in love with a subordinate. And fail the PT test or gain too much weight, and you risk getting the boot. For cadets, grades are huge. The Army doesn't want you if you can't keep a 2.0. And get caught using a fake ID to buy booze and you're out.

With all these ways to fail, everyone's at risk. And sometimes it's the ones you never expect who fall the hardest.

Like Griggs. She was battalion commander of her Junior ROTC unit in high school. The way she walks, the way she talks, her smile, and the gleam in her eyes—everything about the girl barks confidence and command. She fell in love with USC when she saw its lush lawn ringed with nineteenth-century buildings while on a tour of Carolina colleges with her southern-born mom. She joined ROTC because she wants to fly Apaches and get her Airborne wings. So it isn't luck or a privilege when she gets accepted to Airborne School, it's her due. And it's with all confidence in her ability to complete the training that Lieutenant Colonel Moring and Sergeants Bell and Blaylock send Griggs to Fort Benning the summer after her freshman year.

But nobody counted on the pull-up.

On one of the first mornings of Airborne School, after push-ups, sit-ups, and a two-mile run, the sergeants Airborne line up the legs in front of the pull-up bars and give them all two seconds to go from hanging to chin over the bar. One by one, the other legs do their pull-ups and move out. Then it's Griggs's turn. She grabs the bar, hangs with her arms straight, and commands her muscles to *lift*.

But nothing happens.

Now, Griggs is a PT stud. Really. A high school soccer star, she outruns most of the female cadets and many of the males. When Fauth is sucking wind, trying to make the 15:30 perfect time on her two-mile run, it's Griggs who jogs out to pace her. She's a sports therapy major, required to take weight training for her degree, and she often invites other cadets to work out with her class. As a freshman, she's got the third-best PT score of any female in ROTC, seasoned juniors and seniors included. But for some reason, she's no damn good at pull-ups. And at Airborne School, pull-ups are important. If you're lying on the ground after a hard landing and the wind fills your parachute, inability to pull up on your risers and unhook your harness may mean getting dragged miles and miles on rough terrain, perhaps to your death. No joke, it's happened before.

So there she is, hanging on that lonely bar, pulling with all her might and getting nowhere. One second passes. She relaxes, then strains again. Nothing, and now two seconds are up. Sergeant Airborne barks at her to get off the bars. Just like that, Griggs has failed Airborne School, embarrassed her colonel and her trainers, disappointed all those cadets who thought she was a leader, and blighted her nascent career. From here on out, she's "the one who failed Airborne."

And to make matters worse, Fort Benning isn't done with her yet. Normally when someone fails out of a school or otherwise finds themselves with time on their hands, the Army puts them to work shoveling food in the chow hall or plucking weeds from the gravel-paved training areas. It's called "detail," and it's a soldier's customized hell. But for some reason, nobody ever gets around to assigning Griggs and her fellow Airborne flunkies any work. Instead they're crammed in a classroom in the basement of an old building and told to watch DVDs on the big-screen TV. Which they do for two weeks straight. Every once in a while, an officer or an NCO pokes their head into the room to make sure nobody is sleeping. They're failures, damn it, and this is their punishment, bizarre and pointless though it may be.

Half-asleep on her third viewing of the same episode of *Family Guy*, Griggs thinks about pull-ups and what went wrong. As best as she can figure, all those years of soccer have given her a strong lower body at the expense of her arms and back. She can do push-ups like a champ, but that's because she does a lot of push-ups: hundreds per day at the peak of the Ranger Challenge season. Pull-ups on the other hand are no fun and rarely a part of PT. All you need to do push-ups is a piece of real estate and gravity. But pull-ups require expensive and bulky equipment, so of course ROTC neglects them. Besides, the pull-up is such an unnatural motion. In what bizarre circumstances would you ever need to *pull* your entire body *up* using only your arms?

In a parachute harness, is the answer. Too bad there's not more parachuting at college.

Day after day, DVD after DVD, Griggs wastes away in that Fort Benning basement. When she's pondered the pull-up past the point of exhaustion, her mind turns inward and backward. She thinks about growing up in Harrisburg, Pennsylvania, with her mom. She thinks about her high school—with 1,200 students, the biggest thing in a small town. She thinks about being one of only a couple dozen blacks in the whole school. She thinks about the day her history teacher brought in those old photos of his own war experiences, and how she was fascinated by the uniforms, equipment, and exotic faces and places in the pictures. She decided right then and there that she was going to enlist in the military. And when her high school offered Junior ROTC her senior year, Griggs was the first in line to sign up.

One day she told her mom about her military aspirations. Griggs wasn't sure what she'd expected, but it wasn't this. Neither pleased nor displeased, Mom sat her down and told her matter-of-factly about her brother, Griggs's uncle, a Marine who had died in combat in Vietnam. "If you want to be a soldier, I support you," said Mom. "But I don't want you enlisting before you give college a try."

But Griggs never quite let go of her enlisted dream. Several cadets in the Gamecock Battalion are also members of the Army Reserve or National Guard through a program called Simultaneous Membership. Take MSIII Scott Young, for instance. He's a sergeant in a National Guard tank battalion. Get him talking and he'll describe the way a seventy-ton tank feels, sounds, and smells as it churns up the landscape. He'll tell you how the main cannon is so powerful that every time it fires, it forces sheets of microscopic dust through the seams in the tank's shellproof armor, blinding you if you're dumb enough to keep your eyes open. Simultaneous Membership program cadets like Young take classes, train with ROTC, and spend weekends and summers with their reserve units. The Army pays their tuition through the GI Bill and promises them that they won't be deployed as long as they're students. And when they graduate, they get commissioned and surrender their enlisted rank.

To Griggs, this is the way to go. And when Moring informed her freshman year that scholarship funds were tight and Griggs might not get much money from ROTC, it sealed the deal. She approached a local recruiter and told him she wanted to enlist.

She looked forward to boot camp, to getting sweaty, dirty, and abused by tough-love drill sergeants. She looked forward to the camaraderie of suffering with fellow recruits. Finally she'd have the same kinds of memories and mementos that her history teacher so cherished.

But Moring wasn't about to let her go so easily. He didn't want one of his best cadets sharing her time with the Army Reserve. So he promised to give her the first scholarship he could find, *and* he promised her an Airborne slot.

Griggs wavered. Damn, she wanted to go to Airborne, and it was notoriously difficult for enlisted troops to get in. She'd just about made up her mind to accept Moring's offer when a scholarship became available. But rather than give it to Griggs as he'd promised, Moring handed it to some female grad student track star.

Griggs was furious. She marched straight to her recruiter to sign, date, and make her enlistment official. But unknown to her, the colonel had foreseen just such a contingency, and when a second scholarship came up, he immediately assigned it to Griggs without even asking her if she still wanted it. And since ROTC takes precedence over the Reserve, Griggs's recruiter had no choice but to cancel her enlistment.

Her enlisted dream was dead. On the bright side, she had a scholarship now. And she was on her way to Airborne School.

Things were looking up.

Up.

Up.

Up.

Since when is such a simple concept so difficult to execute? All she had to do was *pull herself up* just a few inches. Just once! If she'd managed to get her chin over that bar, everything would be perfect. She'd be in jump week, harnessing up and hurling herself out of the sides of C-130s. She'd be *this close* to being Airborne, to winning the approval of her colonel and her trainers and the respect of her peers. She'd be well on her way to duplicating Fauth's performance as a high-speed female cadet and maybe even becoming battalion commander herself in a couple years. That'd be the final step before commissioning as an aviator and heading to Fort Rucker to fly Apaches.

Instead she's watching a bad remake of *The Texas Chain Saw Massacre* in the basement with a bunch of rejects. And when Fort Benning finally lets her go, she gets a call from the colonel. Needless to say, he's pissed. He wants Griggs to come back to USC so he can chew her out in person.

"You're crazy if you think I'm coming all that way for a five-minute meeting," she says. "I'll see you later."

She hangs up. She packs up. She catches a flight to Charlotte to see her sister. And for the next several weeks, she relaxes, goes out with her sister, and thinks about her past, her present, and how she can salvage her future.

Whether she knows it or not, that's what sets Griggs apart from her peers. She's not the first cadet to fail spectacularly. Nor will she be the last. But where magnificent failure makes most people curl up, clam up, and withdraw, the Great Pull-up Disaster of '04 just makes Griggs harder, meaner, and more determined than ever to be the best soldier she can be.

She's got a PT plan. She's going to work on her sit-ups and improve her run still further, to 14:30 for two miles. And, of course, she's going to focus on pull-ups. She'll study hard, drink less, and try to make more friends in ROTC. She won't cry when Sergeant Bell shuts the door behind himself and spends the better part of an hour listing her inadequacies, all of which seem to have appeared in the wake of that fateful pull-up. And she won't even flinch when Sergeant Blaylock sees her walking down the hall and yells in front of everyone, "You made a fool of me, Griggs!"

Because she's a survivor. And for all of her fantasies about boot camp and life as one of the lower enlisted, Griggs has no desire to be enlisted as punishment. The whole point is to *choose*, to *volunteer*, to walk up to that recruiter and say, "I want to be a soldier." Forced enlistment is a slap in the face, and one the Army delivers surprisingly often. Misbehaving West Pointers, cadets caught cheating, those in ROTC who violate any clause of their contracts with the Army—they're made to enlist as privates and serve out at least as many years as they stole from the Army. In the history of the Gamecock Battalion there have been plenty of forced enlistments. Just last year a cadet was kicked out and forced to enlist, and he soon found himself on a plane to Iraq.

He deserved it. He had an affair with one of the military science department's (married) civilian secretaries, the same secretary one of the sergeants in the unit had *his* eye on. The two suitors almost got into a fistfight. The sergeant was promptly transferred out, and the cadet ended up an unhappy private sweating and stomping camel spiders in Iraq. As for the woman? She just kept right on keeping on. A year later she's still filing paperwork and taking calls for the colonel.

Failure, it seems, is a fickle bitch. But never fear. If you're bound and determined to screw up, you'll find a way. From where Griggs is standing, it seems some cadets actually *want* to fuck up. Take for example the cadet who gets hammered the night before the first PT test of 2004 and nearly passes out after a couple of laps around the track the next morning. They have to call an ambulance for the poor fool. Later the new training NCO, Sergeant Major Connette, hands out some collective ass-chewing in the form of a little story. It's about a sergeant first class he once knew, a real snake-eating hard-ass who loved the Army as much as he loved his men. He took some shrapnel in battle but kept right on fighting.

Connette's eyes grow wide. "Can you live up to that?" he says.

He tells the cadets how it's going to be. No more showing up to PT smelling of alcohol. (Well *that* eliminates a quarter of the battalion, Griggs thinks.) And, adds Connette, no more flunking out of schools.

Schools like Airborne.

Ouch. He may as well have slapped Griggs in the face. And it only gets worse. Leveling his gaze at the ranks of terrified cadets, Connette gathers every shred of contempt he's squirreled away in almost twenty years in the real Army and says, "You disgust me."

It's not how Moring would have addressed the issue, but it works all the same. This is an Army at war, is what Connette is saying in so many colorful words. And make no mistake, every cadet in attendance sees his point: shape up or ship out and die in Iraq.

Lies My Leaders Told Me

It's May 2003, and President George W. Bush is on top of the world. His army has conquered Iraq in three weeks flat, even without the help of a large coalition. Successful military campaigns are also underway in Afghanistan, the Philippines, and on the Horn of Africa. Libya, supposedly quaking at the prospect of an Iraq-style American blitzkrieg, has voluntary suspended its chemical weapons program. The economy is on the rebound. The president's approval ratings are on the rise. And he's scored a sweet photo-op landing on the aircraft carrier *Lincoln* dressed in a crotch-tastic flight suit and flashing his signature thumbs-up for audiences worldwide.

Yessiree, Bush is feeling good. And to end the season on a high note, he stops by the University of South Carolina on May 9 to inject some gravitas into his foreign policy—and while he's at it, to bask in the warm glow of high-brow patriotism at this, the most Bush-friendly school on the planet. Nowhere is the President guaranteed a more positive reception of his speech. Published transcripts end up looking like this:

> We will use our influence and idealism to replace old hatreds with new hopes across the Middle East. (*Applause.*) A time of historic opportunity has arrived. (*Applause.*) A dictator in Iraq has been removed from power. (*Applause.*) The terrorists of that region are now seeing their fate. (*Applause.*)

The president's visit is a coup for Gamecock Battalion. In the weeks preceding and following May 9, awareness of ROTC is at an all-time high. People notice when cadets are around. There are more respectful nods and envious glances. It's hard to quantify, sure, but just as hard to ignore. The vibe peaks in the President's speech, when he offers a shout-out to all the cadets: "For those of you who are going into the ROTC, you will be entering a military that will remain second to none." For a brief shining moment, there's no better thing to be than a soldier, even a part-time pseudosoldier like Cadet Jerry Banfield.

But Banfield's not feeling it. All of this patriotic hoopla just makes him nervous. Watching the news and reading the paper, he sees something lurking underneath the victories, speeches, and positive approval ratings. He sees a nation hurtling headlong toward disaster. And it scares him.

He should have seen it coming. Banfield's a guy who believes in things. He believes in right. He believes in wrong. He believes in signs. And at least twice in the past year, there have been signs that not everything was right in the world. The first was in the fall, on the first night of his very first FTX. The truth is, he was having a blast running around in the woods with a rifle, eating MREs, peeing on stumps, and sleeping in creepy old barracks.

His platoon had settled into the barracks for a few hours of sleep before the next mission. The old building was lined with two-tiered bunk beds. Banfield wound up on top, breathing the hot stale air rising off the floor. Rather than mess with sheets, everyone slept in their sleeping bags atop the old mattresses. It was crude, and the Reagan-era sleeping bags smelled like mothballs. But after a day of traipsing through the woods and playing GI Joe, Banfield was exhausted. He was fast asleep within seconds of settling in.

And the next thing he knew, he was lying on the cement floor hurting all over. It took him a moment to figure out that he had rolled right out of bed and fallen six or seven feet to the ground. The slap of limp Banfield on concrete had awoken everyone. All around the barracks, cadets were sitting up, groggy and disoriented. It took only a few seconds for them to orient on the source of the sound and see Banfield sitting on the floor in a daze. Someone sniggered. Someone else guffawed. Then the whole barracks broke out in loud snorts and sleepy giggles.

In retrospect, Banfield realizes he missed the symbolism of his fall. A young cadet asleep in the stifling darkness unconsciously escapes his soft and lofty perch and tumbles to the hard unforgiving reality, far below. It's funny, sure. More important, it's *eye-opening*.

The next symbol was less ambiguous. On the spring FTX, Banfield was assigned to a squad led by an overconfident junior. It was Sunday. There was just one mission left: a raid on an enemy outpost just a few kilometers away. After that, a barbeque with hamburgers, hot dogs, and cold drinks. It was all anyone could think about.

The mission should have been easy. It was all but a straight line from their starting point to the enemy outpost. But the old adage about cadets with compasses again rang true. Soon Banfield's squad was lost and getting loster. But the junior in charge refused to admit it and marched confidently ahead despite mounting indications that they were entire grid-squares off course, namely the thick tangle of thorns that seemed to have sprung from the earth all around them.

With every step the thorns grew thicker and visibility decreased. Soon the only way they could stay together was to line up back to chest and shove forward like a human locomotive. By now turning back was pointless. It certainly couldn't get any *more* congested, could it?

The thorns grabbed patches and sleeves and straps. More than once, cadets fell to the ground, dragging their peers down with them and threatening to derail the entire train. Thorns sliced shins and forearms and impaled fingers. Cadets winced, yelped, swore, and bled. All the squad leader could do now was set his jaw, ignore the mounting discontent in the ranks, and keep on keeping on. Eventually they would break free. Eventually they would find their way. Eventually everything would work out for the best.

Right?

Wrong. Now Banfield understands what fate was trying to tell him. That thicket was a metaphor for the war on terror. And his squad was just the U.S. Army in miniature. President Bush has ordered Banfield's Army into an inescapable field of thorns, where it will become hopelessly lost. Every roadside bombing and sniper attack will bleed it and sap its strength, but it will just dumbly press on, confident that somehow everything will work out.

But it won't. Not this time.

Banfield's been a cadet barely two years when he decides he's got to get out.

He's scared—not of his trainers and peers, but of his parents. His dad is ex-Army. His mom is an Army veterinarian. For two summers Banfield has interned at her office. More than anything, Banfield is scared that leaving ROTC will mean disappointing his parents.

To his surprise, when he confesses his decision, his parents are *relieved.* It turns out they share his growing disillusionment. In fact, Banfield's dad has always harbored the same sentiment. A Vietnam vet with some bad, bad memories rattling around his head, he's always kept his reservations to himself. After all, the Army's been a good patron. It's given his wife a chance to do what she loves, and it's paid for his son's education. But it's impossible to ignore anymore the institution's decay. It started at the top, with the corrupt Vietnam-dodging commander in thief. And it's trickled down all the way to ROTC, where blandly smiling lieutenant colonels wax lyrical about service and sacrifice and ignore the cold, hard reality that Americans are dying on a daily basis for a cause that's dubious at best and criminal at worst. And it's going to get worse before it gets better.

Time is running out. Cadets without scholarships can try ROTC commitment free for as long as two years. On the first day of their junior years, they sign a contract to serve eight years in the U.S. Army, one way or another. Most cadets earn their commissions and serve out their obligations as officers. Contracted cadets—juniors and seniors as well as underclassmen with scholarships —still owe eight years if they flunk out, quit, or get the boot. Sometimes the Army forces them to enlist. Sometimes it lets them buy their way out of their commitment, often to the tune of $20,000 or more. On occasion the Army just throws them in prison. With his junior year looming, Banfield knows he has to make his move. He's in Legare one day, talking to the cadre, when a major casually mentions contracting.

Banfield clears his throat. "Yeah, about that. I, uh, think I'm getting out."

The major's face falls. He looks *sad.* For a crazy moment, Banfield actually feels bad.

Then he gets over it. He leaves Legare a freer and happier man. His nation may mire itself in the third-world morass of Iraq and end up only more vulnerable to terrorists. Its Army may spend itself on a dozen foreign battlefields, sacrificing thousands of young men and women to the imperialistic ambitions of a corrupt president. But one thing is certain: Banfield won't be one of them.

And neither will sophomore Mitch Monroe. Which is ironic, because he kind of likes war.

A lean, scowling, muscular blonde from Virginia, Monroe passed up a $16,000 scholarship to Christopher Newport University back home when Colonel Buchanan, a lifelong Army buddy of Monroe's dad, offered him a four-year scholarship to come to USC. Monroe's older sister was already there; for years Buchanan had been pressing her to join up, promising money, excitement, and relationships to last a lifetime. For some reason his sister never took the bait. Monroe did. He moved to Columbia, enrolled at USC, declared a computer engineering major, and planned out his future.

He was going to branch Aviation. Barring that, he'd go Military Intelligence and try to weasel his way into the Special Forces. How cool would that be? Capt. Mitch Monroe, commando. After couple years of kicking ass all over the planet, he'd settle somewhere nice with his medals, badges, and battle scars and let the Army pay for grad school.

That was the plan. But it was contingent on one thing: getting the damn scholarship. No sooner had Monroe settled in Columbia than Buchanan admitted there'd been a little glitch. The Army had promised more scholarships than it could afford, to the tune of $14 million. Monroe was going to get his scholarship, Buchanan said, but he might have to wait a few months.

Fortunately, Monroe's parents had set aside some money. He shrugged, hunkered down, and got to work, never doubting that what the Army promised, it would deliver, albeit late.

But towards the end of first semester, Monroe began to see signs that maybe this Army wasn't all it claimed to be. For one thing, there was a huge disconnect between the Army's standards and its actual training. Never was this more evident than at the FTX, which to Monroe resembled nothing more than three days of bad slapstick.

During a tactical exercise, a female cadet nearly knocks herself unconscious when she throws herself on the ground and lands face-first on her rifle. There's a proper way to go prone with a weapon, but apparently she's never learned. Some cadets roll their eyes and blame the dumb bitch. Monroe blames whoever trained, or failed to train, the dumb bitch.

On the land nav course, an MSIII cadet leads a squad of underclassmen hundreds of meters off course, which he blames on a malfunctioning magnetic compass, until someone points out that he's holding the compass next to his metal M16.

One of Monroe's cadre catches him wearing a camelback, a slim backpack full of water, and chews him out for using unauthorized equipment. Never mind that the same officer has stressed over and over the importance of staying hydrated. Never mind that everyone in the real Army wears camelbacks, and some units even make them mandatory. "Fine," Monroe says, throwing his canteens and camelback on the ground. "I don't need water." Later the officer apologizes and begs Monroe to please keep hydrating.

At the patrol base one night, the cadet on security falls asleep, and the enemy sneaks in and opens fire. A crazy melee ensues. If it were real, everyone in camp would be dead. The real kicker: the cadet on security sleeps right through the gunfight, and no one even notices until later.

Buchanan continued to promise Monroe a scholarship, but it might be just a few more weeks. A few more weeks turned into a few more months, and a few more months turned into "maybe next year." By the end of his freshman year, Monroe no longer believed anything the Army said.

And his parents were still paying tuition.

Sophomore year rolled around. Monroe still held out some hope of getting a scholarship. Buchanan was a family friend. Surely he'd deliver.

But Buchanan left, and Moring took his place. One of Moring's first acts was to disburse the unit's scholarship money. Guess who didn't get a penny?

Monroe felt betrayed. And it only got worse. Despite the empty promise of a scholarship, Monroe liked Buchanan. He liked the man's bravado and his tough rhetoric. And he liked the way Buchanan did everything in his power to help every cadet do his best, even if the cadet fought him every step along the way. Buchanan wanted cadets to succeed more than even *they* wanted to succeed. But Moring was different. Soon after taking command, he started cleaning house, telling some of the less confident cadets, especially those from satellite schools like Benedict, to shape up or ship out. And if they didn't promptly shape up, Moring kicked them out. He had no patience for reluctance.

Which is funny, because Monroe was feeling mighty reluctant. And it was the Army's fault.

Now it's the spring of 2003, and everyone's getting excited about the military. President Bush lands on the *Lincoln* on May 1st and declares the invasion of Iraq a victory. On May 9, he puts on a garnet-and-black robe and waxes unconvincing about the future of the Middle East before a packed auditorium at USC. For much of the summer, violence in Iraq is at a minimum. Summer turns to fall and fall turns to winter, and everything's under control. November 11 is Veterans Day, the perfect end to the perfect war-mad year.

Veterans Day is a big deal in Columbia. There's a parade down Main Street and everyone's invited. Troops from Fort Jackson are there. Hundreds of military retirees take part. So does every Junior and Senior ROTC unit in town, the Gamecock Battalion included. Everyone gets a haircut and a shave, gets dressed up in their best uniform, and lines up behind their unit's flag. It's supposed to be voluntary, like the military itself.

But the military's not always as voluntary as it claims. In just over six months, with more than one thousand Americans dead and every ground combat unit in the military either returning from, currently in, or getting ready for Iraq, the Department of Defense dips into its deepest reserves, the Individual Ready Reserve, a pool of former soldiers who have left the service early for civilian careers. Few of them ever expected to get called up. Some never even bothered to inform the Army when they moved or changed their names. Like Selective Service—that is, the draft—the IRR was considered a cold-war throwback, a vestige of the eighteen-division Army that stared down millions of Soviet troops across the Iron Curtain and was prepared to take a hundred thousand casualties stopping an armored assault on West Germany.

Well not any more. The post-Soviet, ten-division Army needs men—badly —and the IRR is one of the first places it turns. Thousands of long-retired former soldiers find themselves yanked from civilian life and deployed overseas.

What's more, thousands of service members have been barred from leaving at the ends of their terms by a little-known order called "stop loss," which allows the Department of Defense to retain volunteers beyond their contracts in times of emergency.

Democratic presidential candidate Sen. John Kerry calls stop loss and the IRR call-up a backdoor draft. Defense Secretary Donald Rumsfeld calls them necessary. Jerry Banfield and Mitch Monroe would call them business as usual for a corrupt and deceitful Army.

Maybe Monroe's reading too much into it, but the undoing of the volunteer military seems to trickle down even to ROTC. After insisting for months that the Veterans Day parade is voluntary, just a few days before November 11, the cadre changes its mind and declares it mandatory. Too bad that it's on a

Friday, when some cadets have classes, others have work, and the rest have plans.

Monroe's pissed. He marches down to Legare and leaves a note for Whomever It May Concern, saying that he's very sorry, but he has a class that he just can't miss. Later he gets a serious ass-chewing for daring to defy an order.

It's the final straw. Monroe quits ROTC at about the same time that Banfield does. They're not the only ones to do so. Other cadets quit when faced with the reality of contracting and an eight-year obligation. Still others like the idea of a military career, but just can't seem to balance school, work, ROTC, and basic functions like sleep. Still others perform so poorly that Moring sees them on their ways. That one cadet sleeps with the colonel's secretary and gets sent to Iraq as punishment. All year, every year, cadets come and go. ROTC is like that: a chance to try out the Army for a week, a month, or even two years, without much risk of death or disfigurement. Some try it and love what they see, things like honor, camaraderie, fun, and sweet uniforms.

Others see only things they hate, like incompetent cadets, arbitrary orders, and lying leaders. Folks like Banfield and Monroe leave ROTC frustrated but much wiser, knowing now what President Bush and Monroe's dad knew thirty years ago. The military's just not for them.

The Usual Suspects

Maj. Terry Truett is an aviator on a three-year assignment as the Gamecock Battalion's training officer. It's his job to do the higher-level planning for FTXs and labs; the hands-on stuff the sergeants and MSIVs handle for the most part. But on a foggy Sunday morning on a remote corner of Fort Jackson in September 2004, he's standing atop a thirty-foot rappelling tower with ropes, harnesses, D-rings, and a bunch of scared-shitless MSI, 'II, and 'III cadets wearing Swiss seats.

Hook 'em up, toss 'em off. One by one, he sends forty cadets off his tower—a few more than once. Staring into the cadets' faces as they scuttle down the tower's sloped face towards the sound of the belay man's encouragement ("Keep on coming, cadet! You can do it! High speed!"), Truett tries to match names and faces. Griggs he knows. Rowland, too. And Heron and Gillespie. But who's that shy black girl with the big round eyes? Truett peeks at the cadet's nametape as she breathlessly leans back over the edge of the tower, her back nearly parallel to the sawdust-covered ground.

That's right: Anderson. One of the new freshmen. The fact that he barely recognizes her is a problem, and Truett makes a mental note to keep an eye on the girl.

In the major's experience, a quarter of cadets in a given ROTC unit are truly dedicated. They're the ones who join Ranger Challenge and Rho Tau Chi, the "professional military society" that meets once a month to talk about war and drink sodas. They're the ones who hang around Legare chatting up the cadre or finding ways to help out. Truett calls them ROTC rats. Griggs is one. In fact she's the very model of an ROTC rat, Airborne gaffe notwithstanding. But this Anderson character is no rat.

The colonel has made it his mission to encourage the Griggses and to weed out the Andersons, and Truett totally agrees. It's the seventeenth month of the occupation of Iraq. Casualties are mounting. So is the rhetoric of naysayers and liberals. The Army is growing by 30,000, tightening its budgetary belt, cutting head-in-the-clouds procurement programs, and bracing for the long haul. With a presidential election in November and Iraqi and Afghani elections scheduled for the next few months, the Iraqi insurgency only growing, and the battered Taliban making noise again, the stakes are high and getting higher. It's time that ROTC reflect the hard realism of the wartime Army. Already, only a month into the school year, Moring and his cadre have trimmed the Gamecock Battalion from 130 to fewer than 90 cadets, mostly by scaring off freshmen. But they can probably afford to scare off a few more. After all, the battalion is expected to graduate only twenty cadets per year. And Moring's made it very clear that he'd rather commission fifteen cadets than twenty if the higher number means sacrificing quality or compromising standards.

Taking a break from the rappelling tower, Truett confides with a couple of NCOs. "How's accountability?" he asks.

"The usual suspects," is one sergeant's response. In other words, the cadets who failed to show up at 7:00 this morning are the same cadets who fail to show up on most mornings. Tomorrow, at PT, the MSIVs will have a little chat with them, provided they attend. If the lower-ranking MSIVs can't straighten them out, Fauth will work them over. If *that* doesn't work, the cadre will take a turn. Short of a sit-down with the colonel, the worst thing that the cadre can inflict on the usual suspects is a one-on-one with Sergeant Major Connette, who at this very moment is balancing on two ropes suspended between two towers across the training area from Truett's rappelling station.

Fort Jackson calls this place Victory Tower. Actually it's three towers, one about fifty feet tall in the middle, flanked by two shorter ones. From one of the short towers, Truett directs the short rappel. From the other, Sergeant Aiken sends cadets across a rope bridge to the tall tower, where Connette receives them and kicks them upstairs to Sergeant Bell, who along with Fauth is running the tall rappel station, fifty feet up the vertical face of the tower. For most of the morning, the cadre and the MSIVs run the MSIs, 'IIs, and 'IIIs through a half-dozen stations, swinging on ropes and climbing nets before tackling the short rappel as a warm-up to the tall rappel. Higher's intent for this training event is that cadets have some fun and face their fear of heights. It's also a way of weeding out the cowards and identifying the usual suspects, those cadets whose laziness or drinking habits preclude voluntary training on Sunday mornings.

That's right, voluntary. According to Cadet Command, training on Victory Tower is not required to earn your commission. But like many "voluntary" events in the U.S. Army, attendance is required at the unit level. If your colonel expects you there, then you'd better be there, even if some distant Army command says that it's up to you. Very little is truly voluntary in the U.S.

Army. Doing things you don't necessarily want to do is pretty much what the military is all about.

Truett knows all about it. He never wanted to spend six months in Somalia in 1992 and again in 1993. He didn't want to eat MREs for the entire deployments. He didn't want to get shot at by Somalis with antique rifles and (thankfully) poor aim every time he flew over Mogadishu in his Kiowa scout helicopter. And he didn't really want to go from flying Kiowas and then Blackhawks to manning a desk, and occasionally a rappelling tower, at USC.

But here he is, doing his duty.

It's getting late now—late by Army standards that is. It's almost noon. The sun is high, the air is hot and dry, and the morning fog has long burned away. Standing atop his tower, Bell scans the cadets scurrying below like camouflaged ants.

He spots something peculiar and calls out a cadet's name. "Hey, McEwen!"

The cadet, a short black kid, skids to a halt, snaps into the parade rest position with his hands behind his back (a sign of respect when speaking to NCOs) and hollers out, "Yes, Sergeant?"

"What's that you're wearing?"

"What's what, Sergeant?"

"*That*, Cadet!"

McEwen knows what Bell's talking about, he just doesn't want to admit it. This morning, getting dressed at the crack of dawn after a wild night and only a few hours of sleep, McEwen couldn't find his regulation black belt and didn't feel like trying any harder, so he slipped on a shiny brown patent leather belt, assuming nobody would notice.

Somebody noticed.

"Get down, McEwen," Bell says. By now everyone in the area is watching. Some cadets chuckle, but not too loud. At events like this it's critical to avoid drawing too much attention to yourself. Attention means scrutiny. And since nobody's perfect, especially in a bunch of ROTC cadets, scrutiny means somebody's going to notice your brown belt, your long sideburns, your five o'clock shadow, the sloppy shine on your boots, and the irritated defiant look in your eyes. And that means push-ups. Lots of them.

McEwen hits the sawdust, arms spread, feet together, and face lifted high in the position that Army calls the "front leaning rest."

"Knock 'em out till I say stop," Bell calls. The lilting tone in his voice is a dead giveaway that he's enjoying every second of this.

So is McEwen. For some, punishment is badge of honor, especially for a clown like McEwen. It's proof that you don't take things too seriously. And if you happen to be a PT stud—and if you're going to goof off, you'd better be— it's a chance to show everyone how many push-ups you can do. Besides, you can put McEwen in the front leaning rest all day every day. He's not going to quit on account of some stupid push-ups, however tired he gets.

McEwen *must* be tired. He knocks out around thirty and levers back into the front leaning rest. Honestly, it's not a very restful position. It's just slightly less strenuous than an actual push-up. When your sergeant wants to hurt you, he puts you in the front leaning rest and leaves you there. Which is what Bell does to McEwen. The cadet sweats and grunts, but never stops smiling. Meanwhile, Bell stands atop his tower like a mustachioed pot-bellied Colossus and just laughs and laughs. Finally he tells McEwen to recover and lets him run around for a few minutes believing he's served his sentence, before putting him back into the front leaning rest.

This is just Bell having some fun. He knows he can get away with it because McEwen's the kind of guy who enjoys punishment.

Sitting nearby wearing a safety harness tied to the tower, Fauth rolls her eyes. She doesn't take uniform infractions so lightly. If it were up to her, McEwen's punishment wouldn't be so entertaining for all parties. She'd order him to attention, get in his face, and lose her temper. Nobody enjoys that. Just the other day, Fauth caught an underclassmen hungover at PT and made such a scene about it that Griggs almost had to drag her away.

Today Fauth bites her tongue. Technically she outranks Bell. But in practice the old sergeant may as well be a general. Cadets are just that low on the Army food chain. So Bell's word is gospel, and if he's going to let McEwen get off with just a little playful harassment, then so be it.

Besides, she's got more immediate problems. Anderson has huffed and puffed her way up one of the cargo nets to the top of the tower, and it's her turn to tackle the tall rappel.

Fauth checks Anderson's Swiss seat and hooks the poor terrified girl up to the rope. The cadet battalion commander moves with practiced efficiency. An experienced outdoorswoman, Fauth has mastered as a civilian many of the skills most cadets practice only in the Army: knots, rappelling, and parachuting. She's even got a part-time job running the climbing wall at the university's brand new Strom Thurmond Wellness and Fitness Center, where on odd nights ROTC's intramural soccer team plays matches against vastly superior teams of half-drunk, overweight frat types or bright-eyed Christians from various campus ministries. The ROTC soccer team has never won, even with Griggs, a high school soccer star, scoring a couple of goals per game. Griggs likes to make a distinction between "strong" and "athletic." ROTC cadets, on average, are stronger, faster, and more nimble than any frathlete or intramural Bible-thumper. But that doesn't mean they're athletic. Sports take skill. So does rappelling. And while Anderson may be able to pound out more push-ups, sit-ups, and miles than her civilian friends, when it comes to military skills she's no more qualified than any freshman at USC.

And boy does it show when she scoots to the edge of the tower, looks down, and then looks back at Fauth. Her eyes are like golf balls, and beads of sweat roll down her forehead. There's no way in the world she's going to get hurt, not with Fauth on one end, a senior at the bottom holding the rope ("on belay"), and enough officers and NCOs to staff an infantry company just wandering around smoking, sipping coffee, and yelling at cadets.

But tell that to Anderson.

Fauth uses her most soothing voice to coach the freshman through her first tall rappel. "Step down," she says.

Anderson nods, a quick jerk of the head. The lump in her throat is almost visible. She steps onto a shallow ledge just a few feet down the tall face of the tower. She's got one hand on the rope near her chest and the other on the rope behind her back. Relaxing her back hand lets the rope play out. The idea is to relax that hand and push off the wall with your legs, bounding to the ground in two or three ballistic half-loops.

It's easier said than done. But bounding's not even the hardest part. The trickiest part of rappelling for newbies is working up the courage to lean backwards into open space until you're perpendicular to the tower, trusting the rope and your feet to keep you from falling. Short of jumping out of a perfectly good airplane, this is one of the most unnatural actions cadets will ever take.

"Okay," says Fauth. "Lean back. Straight back."

Anderson nods again and leans just a little, but not enough.

"Straight back," Fauth repeats. "You want to be perpendicular to the tower."

Anderson gulps and leans still further. She gulps audibly. Down below, the belay man cranes his neck and yells something encouraging. Meanwhile Bell glances over to check on Anderson, smiles, and chuckles. From his vantage point atop the short rappel, Truett watches Anderson and calculates the odds that she'll last in ROTC.

To her detriment, she's what you might call "physically timid." And she's a black female.

Anderson's ready. She glances over her shoulder at her belay man. Her voice cracks when she whimpers, "On rappel."

"On belay!" the belay man hollers.

Anderson attempts her first bound. It's not terribly bounding.

To Anderson's credit, she's trying. And if there's one thing that'll guarantee success in ROTC and the military at large, it's willpower. Look at Griggs. A couple of months ago she flunked out of Airborne School. That kind of embarrassment would sink most people. But at this very moment she's crawling up a rope bridge under the watchful eye of Connette before a cheering audience of her peers.

The normal method of traversing Victory Tower's uphill two-rope rope bridge is standing, with your feet on the lower rope and your hands on the upper—and even that's no picnic. (Hence the safety net suspended underneath. Periodically a cadet tumbles from the rope, bounces thrice in the net, and then, per Connette's orders, rolls like a toddler downhill to the short tower to try again.) But Connette has issued a challenge. Anyone who can *crawl* up the bridge gets to take a day off of PT.

Crawling on an uphill rope is like doing horizontal pull-ups. You straddle the line, wrap your arms and legs like a pretzel, and haul with both hands, dragging your weight a few inches at a time the entire thirty-foot distance between the towers. It's hard. So no one was surprised when Griggs said she'd try.

"Try" wasn't the right word. What she meant was that she'd "do" it. There is no try. Not when everyone watching knows her as the girl who failed Airborne. This stupid little rope bridge at stupid little "voluntary" Victory Tower all of the sudden has become Griggs's big comeback. Just last week Connette told Griggs that she disgusted him. Now he's watching her inch up that rope, hands chafing, muscles straining, and rope cutting deep bruises in her thighs and down the middle of her chest. Looking up at Connette, Griggs can see the hard inflexible standards in his unblinking eyes. He doesn't want effort. He doesn't care about "heart." He's not interested in your enthusiasm. What he wants is success. Wars aren't won with good intentions.

Her muscles scream. Her heart races like she's sprinting a mile. Patches of sweat soak through her uniform. The rope sways with each tug, threatening to spill her into the net, embarrass her further, and justify Connette's disgust.

She cannot fail. She will not fail. Pain is no issue. Physics is beside the point. Griggs keeps crawling. Even when the pain turns to numbness and her vision starts to blur, she keeps crawling. And she makes it, of course. She always knew she would.

At the same moment, Anderson completes her last sloppy bound and spills into the sawdust at the base of the tower. She's shaking so badly that her belay man has trouble unhooking her from the rope. A performance like that from anyone else would invite catcalls and push-ups from the grinning tower-top figurine that is Sergeant Bell. But there's no reason to harass Anderson. It's pretty clear to everyone at Victory Tower that the girl's doomed to wash out, sooner or later. Heckling her would be cruel and pointless.

Not that the Gamecock Battalion is entirely lacking in cruelty. Lounging in the shade under a metal shelter, watching underclassmen freak out on rappel or slide off the rope bridge, seniors Scott Young and Daniel Rowland sip water and mock the more self-conscious 'Is and 'IIs. Poking idly around the shelter, Young turns up an old discarded razor.

"You gonna shave your pubes with that?" Rowland asks.

"Hell, no," Young jokes. "I'm not falling for that again."

"You could shave your ass."

"No, I wax that. Girls don't like a hairy ass."

"I wasn't talking about girls."

When everybody has tumbled off of the tall tower at least once and Sergeant Bell has gotten tired of toying with McEwen, the battalion forms into companies, loads into vans, and drives across post to an expansive land nav course. There they break for lunch, ripping into MREs like the most caloric Christmas ever. Sergeant Bell wades through a tangle of cross-legged cadets slurping potatoes au gratin from plastic sleeves, checking his watch, and yelling, "Chow down! You got two minutes!"

Behind a van, some of the seniors surreptitiously unwrap Burger King hamburgers and take enormous shifty-eyed bites, groaning in ecstasy with each exaggerated chew. Just thinking about the prepackaged nastiness of the MREs makes cold fast food taste like Mom's home cooking.

"One minute! Police up your garbage! Top off your canteens! You got formation in thirty seconds!"

There's a flurry of tan MRE plastic as cadets jam their garbage into trash bags and fold and pocket their leftover goodies such as brownies, wheat bread, and five-year-old MRE M&Ms. Pockets bulging, they line up to top off canteens and camelbacks. They're facing three or four hours of land nav under the high Carolina sun; they're going to need water and calories.

A briefing ensues. Freshmen look frightened and attentive. Sophomores fidget. Juniors try hard to not fall asleep standing up. An MSIV delivers an abbreviated OPORD: "Your mission is to find six points using maps and protractors. You've got until 1600. Stick to the roads. Stay with your buddies. Drink water. Don't touch the wildlife. If you cross a highway, you've gone too far. Keep your cell phones handy in case you get lost. Hooah?"

"Hooah."

The MSIVs split the 'Is and 'IIs into teams led by NCOs or 'IVs. Teams of 'IIIs are on their own. At a table beside one of the vans, Fauth hands out coordinates for each team's points. After a few minutes spent locating the points on their maps, the teams head out along an adjacent road. The 'IVs and NCOs playing babysitter hook their thumbs in their pockets and watch smugly as the underclassmen look up the road, down the road, squint at their maps, shrug, and march deliberately if not confidently in a direction they very well may have picked at random. Not exactly land nav, which means following a compass through woods, today's training is more like orienteering—that is, orienting to major landmarks to zero in on your points. It's supposed to be idiot-proof. Hell, half of the points are within sight of the major road bisecting the training range. But even idiot-proof isn't cadet-proof, hence the 'Is' and 'IIs' handlers, not to mention the MSIVs scattered along the road with hints at the ready and full canisters of water for dehydrated cadets who neglected to fill their canteens.

Griggs winds up with Young and some freshman she doesn't know. Off they march in the direction of the northernmost point. The idea is to grab that far point then backtrack to the farthest point on the opposite side of the starting line, picking up all the points in between.

The first point's a good mile away. The three cadets settle into the hip-shifting gait of the heavily-laden, boot-clad soldier, sounding like a plastic marching band, what with the canteens and nylon and Kevlar all two sizes too big and jostling every which way. Young pulls a half-eaten Burger King chicken sandwich from his gear. He looks a little tense and sheepish. "You guys don't mind if I eat this, do you?"

"Naw," is the underclassmen's simultaneous reply.

Young's relieved. He grins and relaxes and munches on his sandwich as he waxes lyrical about his four years as a cadet. Eyeing the clusters of cadets marching up and down the road under close scrutiny by MSIVs and cadre, Young recalls when things weren't so professional. "Once, doing night land nav when I was a freshman, I got back early. I knew if I went back to the assembly area, they'd just put me to work, so I decided to take a nap." He nods at the very field where, three years ago, he curled up with his gear and slept under the South Carolina stars.

Griggs shakes her head in disbelief. But Young's not finished. He chuckles and tells a story about this cadet he knew back in the day. "Tom King was his name. We were always a buddy team. And let me tell you, buddy teams make you stupid." Of course, it didn't help that King had a habit of filling his canteens with tequila or beer. They'd come back from land nav with King staggering drunk.

It hasn't been all drunken fun. Young talks about Advanced Camp, how he injured a knee on the first day then nearly passed out trying to run on it. He collapsed at the APFT and screamed, "Medic!" just like they do in the movies. Rather than send him home, the powers-that-be decided to put Young in a holding company while he healed, in hopes of cycling him through a later session of Advanced Camp. So for six days he sat in a room watching movies and eating, just like Griggs at Airborne. "Gained five pounds," says Young, patting the burgeoning belt of fat around his stomach.

Griggs grimaces sympathetically.

Rolling his eyes and sighing, Young sums up the last four years. "ROTC is great," he says. "Put on high heels, tie your balls in a knot, and hit yourself in the head with a Ping-Pong paddle. That's what it's like."

The freshman looks a little uneasy, like he's not sure how to deal with a senior all of the sudden behaving like a real live person. But Griggs is all smiles. Finally people are starting to act like a family around here. *This* is what she's always wanted.

But not this: just a couple weeks later, she gets a call late at night. It's Sergeant Aiken. "Hello, Kim."

From the strange tone of his voice, Griggs knows before he says it that the sergeant's daughter, the thirteen-year-old with terminal cancer, is dead. For several long seconds, there's silence between them. Then Aiken says, "I better go while I still got my composure." What he doesn't say, what Griggs reads in his tone and imagines on his face is, "Thanks for being a good friend and a good soldier."

X Chromosome Quandary 13

Fauth is an Army woman in every way. She tucks her T-shirts into her jeans. She says "sir" and "ma'am" even to civilians. She doesn't smile too much; she checks with her chain of command before doing anything; and she always sits up straight.

She even looks like an Army woman: of medium height and angular with strong legs and short hair. The best female cadets look like this; skinny women, slight women, they can't handle three-mile road marches with thirty-pound rucksacks. But Fauth ruck-runs with the best of them.

Which is ironic, because ROTC may very well be her last opportunity to run with a rucksack. Women are still barred from most combat jobs in the U.S. Army, and the ones they're not barred from are the less physically intensive, such as those in Aviation, Field Artillery, and Air Defense. Though you might find women from support branches farmed out to infantry and armor units for specific tasks, close-quarters combat, the Army's raison d'être, still belongs to men.

Imagine how all those female ROTC cadets feel. For four years they train side by side with their male counterparts in all the basic skills of infantry fighting. They learn small unit tactics. They train with rifles, grenades, and machine guns. They practice hand-to-hand combat. They sleep in trenches, shit in holes, and rub acne-causing camouflage paint on their faces. But after they get their commissions, they're told that all those things are for men only.

Fauth's Army is half as big as Coe's and McLean's and far less prestigious. The heart and soul of the U.S. Army has always been its fighters, and all of its top leaders hail from Infantry and Armor, both fields denied to women. And while women now make up 15 percent of the Army's officer corps and 20 percent of the entire Army, an increase over the 13-percent-female Army only ten years ago, their prospects aren't improving. The Army is reorganizing to increase the size of its infantry units at the expense of Air Defense, Artillery, and some support jobs, meaning opportunities for women in the Army are getting scarcer even as women in the civilian world demand, and in some cases get, opportunity equal to men.

But this is the Army, and cadets and officers like Fauth are soldiers first and women second, so you won't hear much complaining. Some say job titles are irrelevant in modern warfare, with its shifting front lines and anonymous enemies. As Pvt. Jessica Lynch proved when her maintenance company was ambushed near Nasiriyah, Iraq, in April 2003, women get into combat and suffer just like men. Iraqi insurgents don't care what branch you're in.

Which, some say, is exactly why restrictions on women in combat jobs are archaic. But rather than organize and demonstrate like Europeans and liberals do, Army women just pin up their hair, put on their subdued makeup and sports bras, and go about their jobs. And in subtle ways they vent their frustrations.

Like at Advanced Camp at Fort Lewis, Washington, the final exam of ROTC in the summer after your junior year. At the end of their three weeks at Fort Lewis, cadets rank the dozen members of their squad from first to last. The Army takes into account how your peers ranked you when it decides which branch you'll get. You want a popular branch like Judge Advocate General, Aviation, or Medical? You'd better rank high.

In that way the Army makes cadets subject to their squadmates at Advanced Camp. So if you have it out for another cadet or for his entire sex, camp's a great place to get even. There's a widely circulating rumor in ROTC that the female minority in some squads bands together to form a voting bloc against their male peers. Even if you're the strongest, fastest, smartest, and most conscientious cadet in the Army, if you're a man, your female squadmates are going to rank you low. In fact, the stronger, faster, and smarter you are, the more likely you are to get dinged. The whole point of the conspiracy is to tarnish the Army's golden boys.

Maybe there really are female cadet conspiracies. Maybe they're just myth and paranoia. No one knows because no one's conducted a statistical study of cadets' peer rankings. Still, the perception persists, perpetuated by low-whispering, pissed-off male cadets in cafeterias and dorm rooms late at night.

Cadets shouldn't even know how their peers ranked them. The little cards where everyone scribbles their lists are sealed in envelopes and handed to each cadet to deliver to his commander back at school. But rare is the cadet who resists the temptation to open his envelope on the plane or the bus from Fort Lewis. Rarer still is the cadet, male or female, who speaks openly of what every cadet knows, that in the U.S. Army the sexes are not equal and the resentment between them is real.

Male cadets have their reasons for feeling the way they do. In the field, when a female cadet stumbles under the weight of her rucksack, it's a male cadet who picks her up, helps her out her shoulder straps, and carries two rucks instead of one until the female catches her wind. When somebody falls out of a formation run and trips everybody up, more often than not it's a female. And those females always ruin the fun, frowning on all the sex jokes and shit humor and insisting that men treat women with respect. They're the ones with compassion for the weak. They're the ones who cry when they're in pain and ask for help when they need it.

They're the ones who emote.

Well, most of them emote. Fauth herself is pretty stiff most of the time. But not when she's drinking Guinness and singing bar songs at Delaney's. And not when she's flying.

Fauth graduated from Airborne School in 2003. A senior, she's one of just a handful of cadets with Airborne wings and one of the only females. A lot of Airborne-qualified soldiers enjoy their five jumps, even if the two weeks leading up to jumping are frustrating, boring, and at times painful. But for many the jumps are something to overcome and hardly the kind of thing they would do for fun, or ever again. Many soldiers who go through Airborne School never serve in Airborne units, especially cadets. As often as not, Airborne wings are just prestige items for cadets rather than practical job training.

Fauth's an exception to all the rules. She didn't just enjoy jumping, she *loved* it. And her first thought out of Airborne School was how to get back in that parachute harness.

So when she returned to South Carolina, she started shopping for a skydiving school. She found one in Chester, a small town fifty miles from Columbia. Skydiving, like military parachuting, requires a lot of training. Otherwise they're apples and oranges. Civilian skydivers jump from altitudes as high as 11,000 feet and freefall for as long as forty-five seconds, keeping an eye on the altimeter, and pull their ripcords manually at 4,500 feet. Military parachutists in regular airborne units jump at around 1,000 feet on static lines that automatically deploy their parachutes. A proper landing under a skydiver's square parachute is feather-light. Most static-line jumps result in barely controlled crashes into the ground. A good landing for military parachutists is one that you walk away from.

That's not to say skydiving's not dangerous. Stories of disaster abound. Two jumpers at the Australian National Skydiving Competition ran into each other midair, tangling their parachutes and tumbling to the ground in a knot of limbs and nylon. One jumper walked away okay, but only because he pancaked the other guy, breaking his skull, smashing a lung, and cracking several ribs. And a college kid in Missouri, an experienced skydiver, landed a bit sloppy on an otherwise routine jump, fell onto his face, and promptly died. All told, thirty or forty people die skydiving annually. For her first ten jumps, Fauth was paired with a couple instructor who would hold onto her as they fell, prepared to pull her ripcord if she panicked or screwed up.

But instructors or no, skydiving is the most amazing experience ever. At first it's terrifying, waiting in that plane with your feet firmly planted on something at least, anticipating that most unnatural of states: freefall, touching nothing but your instructors and the rushing wind, for all practical purposes plunging to your doom, relying on a simple machine and basic physics to save your life. Oddly enough, the only time she's ever scared is sitting on the plane. Once she's jumped, once she's confronted the fear head-on, it goes away. Spread-eagle in the open air, she experiences the most curious sensation, one she always struggles to describe. She can feel her body balance, not vertically or even horizontally, but in all dimensions about a single point in her torso. There's her center, her fulcrum and, appropriately enough, her heart. Falling at 120 miles per hour, 10,000 feet above the earth, Fauth is happy.

But she'd be happier jumping alone.

Now it's high summer, 2004, and Fauth is flying again, but this time with the help of a Boeing 737. Behind her is Fort Lewis and the four weeks of boredom and routine that Cadet Command calls Advanced Camp. Ahead of her is Fort Hood, Texas, and something called Cadet Troop Leadership Training, a month-long internship with a military police unit attached to III Corps, the Army's tank-heavy counterattack corps, the most fearsome ass-kickers on the planet, one hundred thousand grinning killers with enough hardware to topple governments in short order.

It's the real Army. And it's everything she hoped it'd be.

For a couple of weeks, Fauth follows around an MP lieutenant. PT at 6:00 A.M. Taskings at 9:00. For military policemen in their law enforcement phase, that means manning checkpoints or patrolling the post—you know, cop stuff.

For MPs in their field phase, those preparing for deployment overseas, it means time on the firing range, squad tactics, and practicing building-clearing techniques on Fort Hood's simulated urban environment, a town complete with roads, houses, tall buildings, and civilians paid to wander around acting like, well, civilians.

The urban training's perhaps the most urgent. Military police companies are some of the most in-demand units in Iraq and Afghanistan. Their flexibility and skills in crowd control and civil matters makes them perfect for dealing with angry populations, thugs, and insurgencies, things Iraq especially has in abundance. Watching those finely tuned MPs crack open a building and tie up its startled occupants in a matter of minutes is awe inspiring and a far cry from the clumsy antics she's used to in ROTC. Nobody gets lost in a thicket. Nobody trips and knocks themselves unconscious with their rifle.

This is what she signed up for. Not Fort Hood, necessarily, since Fauth has always had her heart set on Fort Campbell, home of the 101st Airborne Division. No, it's the sheer professionalism and competence of the MPs that excites Fauth.

But her most memorable experience at Fort Hood isn't even with the MPs. For a week she takes charge of a signal platoon whose lieutenant is temporarily out of commission. In terms of her routine, it's not much different from playing platoon leader in ROTC: formations, operations orders, PT. But in terms of motivation and camaraderie, the signal platoon kicks ROTC's ass hands-down. On a company run one morning, Fauth ends up in front of the formation, setting the pace and leading the way. Someone calls cadence. The company calls back. Everyone's in step. Everyone's excited. When a soldier stumbles, everyone around them helps out. Looking over her shoulder, Fauth sees a hundred soldiers acting and reacting as one. As motivated as the Gamecock Battalion is on its formation runs, this is better by orders of magnitude.

It makes sense. No one here is just "trying out" the Army. No one here is using the Army for scholarship money. No one's here because they couldn't get into their favorite fraternity. And no one's planning on serving their stints as a doctor, a lawyer, or some Adjutant General chairborne ranger. Everyone's a volunteer. Everyone's making far less money than the average civilian. And everyone's going to get deployed to Iraq, where enlisted troops make up the overwhelming majority of fatalities.

Running at the head of that formation, calling cadence with her soldiers, Fauth feels like a real officer, even though she's not. It feels good.

And it only gets better. On a weekend off, she and a lieutenant head to Austin for the social scene. While there they squeeze in a jump at a local skydiving company, where Fauth finally manages to get off of student status so that she can jump alone. Falling towards Texas's brown patchwork with nothing but air all around her, Fauth is on top of the world.

Too bad she can't do *this* for a living. The Army has soldiers who skydive like civilians. In Army parlance, it's called HALO, High Altitude Low Opening, and it's how the Special Forces infiltrates enemy lines without relying on helicopters. Fauth would be perfect for the job. She's tough. She's disciplined. She's smart and motivated and independent, and to top it off, she's already an experienced skydiver.

But she's a she. And women aren't allowed in Special Forces.

Summer Camp Lewis 14

It's hot. It's remote. The food sucks and the folks in charge are plain grumpy. Every summer, thousands of young people flock to a ramshackle camp in the middle of the state of Washington's dense forests for four weeks of supervised activities and hikes through the woods. It's the Army's annual cycle of training for rising senior cadets, the final exam of ROTC. It's called Advanced Camp, and it's like Camp Hiawatha with guns.

But it's pretty damn important as far as summer camp goes. Throughout their first three years of ROTC, cadets earn points. In the fall of their senior year, the Army tallies everyone's points and ranks every senior cadet in the country from first to last to determine who gets the plum jobs. The top cadets get their first choice of assignments, often deferments for law or medical school or active-duty aviation posts. The dregs get stuck with the Chemical Corps or Transportation as glorified truck drivers. Points are important. A perfect score is 3,000; grades, activities, voluntary schools such as Airborne School, and performance at more than three years of weekly training are worth up to 2,000 points. Advanced Camp alone is worth up to 1,000.

So everyone takes it seriously, even though it doesn't take itself very seriously. "Unadvanced Camp," as some cadets call it, can be pretty silly.

Like every school or camp in the Army, the first few days, after everyone arrives by train, plane, or automobile, are dedicated to filling out paperwork, waiting in line for sheets, listening to briefing after endless boring briefing, and getting organized into companies, platoons, and squads. Meanwhile everyone makes the acquaintance of the camp's—ahem—facilities.

Those in the know say Fort Lewis has two halves. One half is like any Army post. There are apartments for the enlisted folks, bungalows for NCOs and junior officers, and nice little houses for the majors and colonels. There's the post exchange, a sort of mini-mall with all the amenities of its civilian counterpart. There's a movie theater, a bowling alley, and plenty of fast food. And of course there are the training areas and firing ranges and motor pools, not to mention a flight line for helicopters.

That's the nice half. The other half of Fort Lewis is all trees, anthills, unimproved trails, and shambling World War II–era barracks.

Guess which half Advanced Camp is at?

The cadets' area is essentially a field ringed with barracks. There's a ghetto-looking basketball court in one corner. In another corner is the dining facility, where, between training, cadets will stuff their faces with the Army's trademark fatty, carb-heavy chow. There's only one Advanced Camp and four thousand cadets to process in just three months, so the Army packs in as many cadets as possible. While one platoon is eating, another's marching, and a third is taking a PT test. Platoons pass in the dining hall or share rides out to events like branch orientation day, a daylong show-and-tell of the Army's favorite toys that's pretty much the highlight of Advanced Camp.

Branch orientation day sees each of the Army's sixteen branches pitch themselves to prospective members. Which branch a cadet goes into is, to an extent, a matter of choice. Not everybody can be an aviator. Somebody's got to fill those slots in the lamer branches. If nobody volunteers for the Chemical Corps, some of the lower-scoring cadets end up getting forcibly volunteered. But no branch is content to settle. Everyone wants the cream of the Cadet Corps crop—and branch orientation is the chance to woo them.

So the Infantry Corps deploys a squad armed with all the latest gizmos. They perform a choreographed attack on a pretend objective, then step up to describe their fancy weapons and gear. Aviation is out there, with presentations on all its different choppers: the sleek Blackhawks, the muscular twin-rotor Chinooks, the bristling Apaches, the nimble little Kiowas. By far the most impressive display is put on by the Field Artillery branch. In fact, they get a whole day to themselves. It's called "fire support day," and it's everybody's favorite.

Cadets pile into buses and drive out to what the artillery calls an "impact range," an enormous firing range pocked with craters and splintered trees and the microscopic remains of unfortunate wildlife. The cadets sit in bleachers and wait. All of a sudden, a Chinook rotors in with a cannon slung underneath. The chopper deposits the cannon and crew then pulls away. In a matter of seconds, the artillerymen have prepared and loaded the cannon. Everyone stands back and covers their ears. A soldier tugs on a cord to fire the cannon.

Boom!

Then the crew gets back to work, packing up the cannon while the Chinook edges overhead. The process is reversed: the artillerymen hook the cannon to the chopper then climb aboard. Only minutes after they appeared overhead, the demonstrators are gone.

It's all very impressive. But it's only the beginning. Next, the cadets take turns calling in artillery fire. They pick coordinates on a map and radio them to a nearby cannon crew, all under the supervision of an experienced officer. Seconds later a shell ripples overhead and makes a big black puff on the range. It's an awe-inspiring and humbling experience to command such destructive power. Never mind that it's all for show, and that it's cadet-proof. It really doesn't matter what coordinates they call in; the cannon's going to shoot at a nice safe spot far downrange. Artillery is far too dangerous to entrust to college students, even college students just a year away from being officers.

Branch orientation is fun. Fire support day is more fun. Otherwise, Advanced Camp is dull, dumb, and demoralizing. And with few exceptions, it's not even hard.

After in-processing, platoons settle into two weeks of what the Army calls "garrison"—that is, nine-to-five life in the barracks. They observe a strict routine, waking before dawn, cleaning the barracks, and making their bunks before lining up in ranks for attendance and PT. After that it's time for chow. Then there's the morning's activities: maybe some marching ("drill and ceremony") or wandering around in the woods trying to find little signs affixed to trees ("land navigation"). Around noon, it's time for chow again. Afterwards, there are more activities like tossing fake grenades at plywood targets or shooting a few rounds at the firing range. At every activity they're observed and rated by recently commissioned lieutenants, folks who just a year ago were themselves prisoners of Advanced Camp and who resent being back so soon.

After several days of garrison, some cadets begin to wonder why they're really here. The cleverer ones like Fauth even figure it out: Advanced Camp's not about marching and shooting and tossing fake grenades. That's just filler. The real point of Advanced Camp is leadership evaluation.

Every day in garrison, leadership positions within each platoon are filled by different cadets. Somebody's the platoon leader, someone else is their sergeant. There are squad leaders and team leaders, too. Every day after dinner, the current leaders rotate out and new cadets take their places. Depending on their specific post, cadets in leadership positions might give briefings, write risk assessments, lead formations, fill out paperwork, and even mete out punishment for minor offenses. Everything they do, every word they write, every sign of weakness or indecisiveness they demonstrate, their evaluators are there, taking notes, drawing conclusions, and preparing to rank cadets against their peers.

Soon garrison draws to a close, and the platoon packs up its rucks for two weeks in the field. Leadership evaluations continue, but under much different circumstances in a simulated combat environment. Not a realistic simulated combat environment, mind you, which in 2003 might involve guarding tedious convoys on booby-trapped roads, navigating blinding sandstorms, manning roadblocks, and conducting low-intensity urban operations in towns packed with restless unemployed locals and poorly trained suicidal insurgents screaming "Allah akhbar!" as they bum-rush you with their antique AK-47s. No, the simulated combat environment of Advanced Camp is a throwback to Vietnam or even World War II: platoon-based combat in wooded terrain against regular infantry that's using much the same tactics as you. Of course, it's tough to fault Advanced Camp when all of ROTC's tactical training is archaic at best and at worst a sick joke whose punch line goes something like, "So this platoon walks into an ambush. . . ."

The local OPFOR, a rotating contingent of National Guardsmen, does its best to make the tactical training at Advanced Camp as irrelevant as possible. For large-scale exercises, everyone is outfitted in Military Integrated Laser Exercise System gear, called MILES for short. MILES consists of a laser emitter fixed to the barrel of your rifle and a series of detectors attached to your helmet and torso. Instead of shooting blanks and yelling "Bang, bang!" cadets at Advanced Camp fire and dodge invisible lasers. The whole point of MILES when it was introduced during the realistic-training revolution of the 1980s was to take the guesswork out of tactical training—and to make it cheat-proof. But given time and incentive, soldiers will find a way to cheat at anything. Twenty years has been plenty long, and the incentive is to teach these officer wannabes a lesson in enlisted wiles. The OPFOR at Advanced Camp is notorious for removing the detectors from their uniforms, making them effectively invulnerable to cadets' fire. And in the hours it takes for lost cadets to land nav their way to the battle, the Guardsmen have time to tune their lasers to near perfection. So while the cadets' lasers fire every which way but straight, the OPFOR never misses. It doesn't help that some enterprising private figured out that if you slap the laser emitter just so, it squirts out a stream of lasers like a magical machine gun, enough to mow down a whole company of bewildered cadets in seconds flat.

Fortunately, Advanced Camp's not really about tactics. Everyone's going to unlearn all that stuff anyway at their respective Officer Basic Courses—or more likely once they join a unit. The point of all the tactical training, like the point those three weeks in garrison, is to give everyone a chance at leadership. And leadership in the field really boils down to two things: giving briefings and maintaining control, which itself means knowing where everyone is and making sure they're doing *something*, however suicidal. A Special Forces major serving as a platoon tac makes it perfectly clear when he says, "I've been in the Army a long time. I'm no infantry expert and neither are you. So I don't care if you assault that bunker from the front. Just stay in control."

Just *lead.*

The most important quality of an Army officer is leadership ability, with all that implies. Advanced Camp is the Army's last chance to evaluate future officers before deciding what to do with them, whether to send them to the Infantry and maybe breed some four-star generals, stick them in one of the technical branches in need of compulsive, analytical types, or consign them to officer purgatory in the Transportation or Chemical Corps.

Perhaps the most important exercise in terms of leadership evaluation is also the silliest. At least billeting and formations and squad tactics look Army. The "Field Leader's Reaction Course," on the other hand, looks like a playground, or the "ropes" course of one of those corporate motivational camps, or one of the challenges on the TV show *Survivor*. The idea is to present a squad leader with an obstacle and a time limit and see how they handle it. Everyone at Advanced Camp gets a chance to lead a squad through the FLRC. Fauth is no exception.

Her challenge is a popular one. Given ten people, some lengths of rope, a dummy simulating a wounded soldier, and a stretcher, get everyone across a sawdust pit without ever touching the ground. At each end of the pits are tall posts that are not unlike telephone poles. The obstacle bears a striking resemblance to the rope bridge event at Ranger Challenge. Squad leaders at the FLRC are given thirty minutes to plan and brief their squads. But Fauth is ready to go in half that time. All she has to do is figure out some way to tie the stretcher to the wire; otherwise it's Ranger Challenge, all over again.

Fauth feels pretty confident. Never mind that the Gamecock Rangers pretty much fucked up their rope bridge at this year's competition. After all, their failure at Ranger Challenge was a technicality: tying their Swiss seats to a different standard then Fort Jackson's. Advanced Camp has no Swiss seat standard.

On the other hand, most of Fauth's squad has never competed in Ranger Challenge and has never tied a Swiss seat, or any knot for that matter. After thirty minutes to prepare a plan, Fauth has another thirty minutes to execute it. It's pretty clear after only a few minutes that she's not going to get everyone across in time. Fauth has to take everyone through the steps to tying a Swiss seat one knot at a time. She has to jury-rig a harness for the stretcher and its dummy occupant then talk two people across pulling the stretcher one foot at a time. In addition to coaxing her entire squad across the obstacle, she has to cross herself. Without her highly trained Ranger Challenge teammates, the whole process is a great deal slower and more awkward than she imagined.

Fauth finishes over the thirty-minute deadline. Her grader is not pleased. As he lectures her on the importance of accurately assessing the difficulty of a task and planning appropriately, Fauth wracks her brain for some way she could have finished in time. But considering the quality and preparedness of her teammates, for the life of her she can't imagine doing it any faster. Hell, McLean had the same obstacle a year ago, and he finished in plenty of time. Maybe he had better cadets.

It's not her fault. But then it *is* her responsibility. In the U.S. Army leaders are responsible for everything that happens under their command, both successes and failures. If your troops excel, with or without your encouragement, you win medals. If your troops screw up—say, take photos of themselves harassing detainees at the prison camp you command—you take the fall.

At least you're supposed to. In May 2003 Brig. Gen. Janis Karpinski, commander of the brigade overseeing Iraq's prisons, refused to accept responsibility for the fiasco at Abu Ghraib and blamed the whole thing on some unnamed CIA types directing interrogation at the prison. Karpinski was suspended from her post anyway and shipped off to Fort Jackson to rot in some minor administrative post. And throughout the Army, soldiers cursed her name, not for letting troops abuse Iraqis detainees, but for ducking the blame.

Fauth is determined *not* to be a Karpinski. She verbally accepts full responsibility for her squad's failure to cross the obstacle in time. Thus she fails the challenge but passes the test. For Advanced Camp isn't an exam in building rope bridges any more than it's an exam in tactics or physical fitness. It's an exam in leadership. And inasmuch as leadership means swallowing your pride and taking the blame for your troops' failures, what the Army calls "accountability," Fauth passes with highest marks.

So when she returns to USC in August to take (cadet) command of the Gamecock Battalion, she's confident that when accessions are announced in December she'll get her top choices as far as branch and duty station are concerned.

Her immediate future in the Army is secure. Now she can turn her attention to more immediate concerns. For in late August, twenty thousand students converge on Columbia for the new school year. Veteran cadets return from various camps and schools. Others are fresh from three months on the beach or bone-weary from working three part-time jobs to pay for tuition. And in addition to the dozens of sophomores, juniors, and seniors, there are scores of wide-eyed freshmen, some arriving with four-year scholarships from the Army, others with years of JROTC under their belts, and still others simply curious about the Army and what it means to them.

Same old thing with some new faces. It's another year in USC ROTC.

War Stories 15

While Fauth is at Fort Lewis negotiating rope bridges and Griggs is at Fort Benning failing to do a single pull-up, Capt. Alan Wilson, a South Carolinian and an officer in the 3rd Battalion of the 178th Field Artillery Regiment, is patrolling the border between Turkey and Iraq, keeping an eye out for smugglers and insurgents.

Wilson's unit, part of the S.C. National Guard, left its rocket launchers behind when it deployed to northern Iraq in February 2004, where it joined another artillery battalion near the Turkish border. It's duty short on combat and long on uneventful patrols and civil-affairs operations such as handing out medicine, overseeing construction projects, and making friends of the local populace. In the summer of 2004 the unit and its parent regiment guard Iraqi laborers working at a former air base, organize a drive back home to supply second-hand backpacks to Iraqi school children, and dig a well for a village outside Nasiriyah that has been drinking from a dirty duck pond. In a season when most Americans hear about only death and destruction in the Sunni parts of the country, Wilson and his soldiers are making friends and progress in Kurd-dominated northern Iraq.

It's been one surprise after another. Before deploying, Wilson fully expected his stint in Iraq to be one riot and ambush after another. But the natives are friendly, even too friendly, always extending invitations to tea and lunch that Wilson and his troops can rarely accept. If anything, Wilson's deployment has been a lot like his life back home, waking early, working twelve hours a day, doing a lot of driving and talking to "customers" and reporting to the boss, and then taking a few hours at the end of the day to jog or work out. His biggest complaint is that he has to wear the same outfit every day.

Just goes to show you, he thinks. Life—and war—is rarely what you expect. ROTC just proves it. For four years he was a cadet. Almost everyone around him was a cadet, too. He sort of got used to the half-assed cadet way of doing things. So of course there was this "oh crap" moment when he stood in front of a bunch of real soldiers for the first time.

But it's all worked out just fine. And it's still working out just fine. Even war isn't as hard as everyone makes it out to be. In six months, Wilson's unit has suffered not a single casualty. When he hears about all the violence and bloodshed in Baghdad, Najaf, and Fallujah, it sounds like it's happening in another country. Wilson's Iraq is not the Iraq he sees on CNN.

Maybe he's just lucky. By November 2004, thirty South Carolinians have died in Iraq and Afghanistan. Three of the dead came from one high school, Orangeburg-Wilkinson, just thirty miles from Columbia, a large school in a poor black neighborhood. It may not be terribly scientific or even fair to draw conclusions from the relative poverty of the community around Orangeburg-Wilkinson versus Wilson's milieu, but it is tempting.

Wilson, son of Republican congressman Joe Wilson, attended Francis Marion College in Florence, South Carolina, and trained with the Gamecock Battalion. After graduating with a history degree and branching Field Artillery, he joined the National Guard and settled in Columbia to attend USC Law school. He was practicing law in nearby Lexington when his unit was called to active duty.

Of the one thousand American war dead as of September 2004, only ninety are officers. Thus officers, who account for around 15 percent of Army manpower, comprise less than 10 percent of its dead. The most quantifiable difference between officers and enlisted is education: officers have degrees. In light of officers' casualty rate, you could say that a college education will cut in half your chances of dying in Iraq. Inasmuch as being an officer shelters him from the bloody infantry combat gobbling up a dozen soldiers a week, Wilson owes his safety to ROTC.

On the other hand, if he weren't in the Army in the first place, he wouldn't be in a position to be gobbled up at all. But if you insist on donning that uniform and sauntering into a war zone—for God, country, or whatever—you may as well do it at an officer's pay and an officer's death rate.

But being an officer, while safer than being enlisted, doesn't make you immune. Just ask the family of Capt. Kimberley Hampton, a 1998 ROTC grad from Presbyterian College, a tiny liberal arts college in Clinton, South Carolina, fifty miles from Columbia. Presbyterian cadets do much of their training at Fort Jackson. And every year they square off against USC at Ranger Challenge.

On January 2, twenty-seven-year-old Hampton is doing what she loves most: flying a helicopter for the U.S. Army.

It's a cool afternoon over the city of Fallujah. Hampton, an Easley, South Carolina, resident fresh from a deployment to Afghanistan, is flying cover for

82nd Airborne Division paratroopers fighting militants holed up in the city. As her twin-seat Kiowa scout helicopter banks over a plantation surrounded by houses, a missile reaches into the sky and strikes the chopper. Hampton's Kiowa spirals to the ground and crashes on the plantation. She's killed instantly, her neck snapped by the impact, and her copilot is wounded. Without hesitating, the paratroopers on the ground surround the crash site, evacuate Hampton's body and the wounded copilot, and then fan out to look for the shooter.

They've done this before.

Hampton's Kiowa is one of more than fifty American helicopters lost in Iraq since the invasion. Hampton is the 593rd American, the first female pilot, the first South Carolina ROTC grad, and the first woman from South Carolina to die in Iraq.

In the weeks following Hampton's death, all that her family can talk about is how proud they are of her. "Kimberly was doing what she wanted to do," her father Dean says. "She believed in the cause; we still do."

And more than eighteen months after the invasion, so do most South Carolinians, cost be damned. More than 1,200 attend Hampton's funeral in Easley. An honor guard from the 82nd marches behind her flag-draped coffin on a horse-drawn caisson. Leading the procession is a riderless black horse, the traditional symbol of a fallen warrior. Meanwhile at Presbyterian College there's a moment of silence at a men's basketball game to remember the star pupil and undefeated tennis champ.

Halfway around the world, 1st Lt. Jon Alexander, commander of the S.C. Guard's 1052nd Transportation Company, is in Kuwait, preparing to head north with his troops, when he receives word of Hampton's death. He and Hampton were classmates and two of only four cadets to graduate from Presbyterian in 1998.

The news is sobering, especially in light of Alexander's mission to oversee supply convoys on some of Iraq's most dangerous roads. Within weeks, the 1052nd has moved into a tent city at a logistics hub called Anaconda, near the town of Balad, north of Baghdad. Every day hundreds of convoys leave Anaconda for every corner of Iraq. And every day twenty of them come under attack. Some of the attacks are decidedly amateurish: kids throwing rocks, local farmers taking potshots with antique rifles. But every once in a while the insurgents get their act together.

Like in April, a month that sees riots and coordinated attacks across occupied Iraq. The media labels it the "Easter uprising." Alexander calls it "when the war got shitty." More than 130 American die in Iraq in April versus fewer than sixty in March. Until early April the 1052nd runs supplies to places like Baghdad in unarmored flatbed trucks with little escort. It takes only a couple rocket attacks to change their ways. Alexander orders his maintenance guys to weld steel onto the trucks' cabs, and he requisitions armored Humvees, equips them with .50-caliber machine guns, and sprinkles them among the trucks in every convoy. Now when they come under attack, the 1052nd opens fire from the Humvees and hits the gas, speeding away from danger at up to sixty miles per hour. Alexander likens it to a NASCAR race with (more) gunfire. Amazingly, despite dozens of ambushes by insurgents wielding rockets and machine guns and planting roadside bombs and despite longer days offering more opportunities to attack, none of Alexander's soldiers are killed in the summer of 2004.

Then comes October, Fallujah, and Ramadan. Thousands of insurgents have holed up in Fallujah during the Muslim holy month. Marines and soldiers are tightening the noose around the city, preparing for an all-out assault. Daily convoys bring weapons and supplies to the assault force. The convoys route through Baghdad, which has seen a spike in riots and attacks as tension mounts across the country.

Alexander rides shotgun in a flatbed, on a mission led by one of his lieutenants. He doesn't have to do it—his responsibilities are more administrative than combat—but he likes to prove that he's a regular joe, that he's willing to take risks alongside his soldiers. And in light of the 1052nd's racial makeup— mostly white in the upper ranks, mostly black in the lower, with a lot of distrust in between—gestures like this are critical. In ROTC it's often said that leadership means facing the same dangers your soldiers face. That's an inspiring platitude when you're sitting in a classroom at USC or Presbyterian. But out here it means sitting in the sweltering heat in a noisy, rattling flatbed, clutching an M16, and nervously eyeing the road as you speed through Baghdad hauling a trailer weighed down by tons of ammunition that will go up like the world's biggest firework if you get hit. It means knowing that at any second, a rocket could pierce your cab and blow you to pieces, a bomb could explode and burst your eardrums and pepper you with shrapnel, or machine-gun rounds could poke holes in your body armor and turn you into ground beef inside.

It's ROTC bullshit made real.

Near Baghdad the convoy gets hit. But no one is hurt, everyone does what they're supposed to, and they speed right through the attack with machine guns blazing. The 1052nd's luck holds for a few more days, until October 27, when a suicide bomber on a motorcycle detonates his load of explosives alongside Staff Sgt. Jerome Lemon's armored flatbed just a few miles outside Anaconda's gate. The explosion tears Lemon's head right off his body and leaves it lying on the floorboards.

Deaths such as Lemon's have become a routine part of convoy operations out of Anaconda. Most of the transportation companies at the base, the majority of which are from the National Guard, lose two or three soldiers to roadside attacks. By the time they come home in February 2005, every driver in the

1052nd has a story about getting attacked. Even Alexander has his close call. But where his enlisted soldiers end their deployments with as many as one hundred missions under their belts, Alexander boasts just a handful, including the October mission. For the most part his duties keep him safely indoors at Anaconda, where the biggest danger is infrequent and inaccurate mortar attacks.

Which is not to say that Alexander's having fun. By no means. Anaconda is hot and dusty in the summer and cold and muddy in the winter. There's not much to do in your off hours. And the chow is, well, typical Army. Straight out of college, Alexander deployed to Kosovo with the 3rd Infantry Division. *That* was fun. Iraq is not. And if you had asked him at graduation, Iraq is the last place he thought he'd wind up.

Alexander commissioned into the Ordnance Corps, the branch of the Army that handles repairs and supplies. But family connections brought him into the S.C. Guard, which was in need of a company commander for the 1052nd. So Alexander, the ordnance officer, wound up commanding a transportation unit of the type that hauls the stuff the ordnance folks work with. Even now, after a year in Iraq with the 1052nd, Alexander shakes his head and laughs when he thinks about his twisted path to command and to war.

As the 1052nd leaves Iraq in early 2005, another S.C. Guard unit, with several ROTC grads in command, gears up for its own yearlong deployment. The 1st Battalion of the 178th Field Artillery Regiment, the 3/178th's sister battalion, deploys to Kuwait—again without its artillery—from where it runs escort missions for transportation companies like the 1052nd.

It's dangerous duty. By 2005, roadside attacks on convoys and their escorts have become one the biggest killers of Americans in Iraq. The war that so many people thought would end swiftly and decisively in America's favor has turned into a deadly, day-to-day slog on Iraq's dusty, lonely roads.

Great Commissioning 16

It's one of the hottest days of the hottest month in one of the hottest states of the former Confederacy. On August 10, 2004, in a tiny room deep inside the sprawling Russell House student union, mothers fan themselves like fat hummingbirds, irritable children squirm in uncles' laps, stoic father-types try hard not to look like they're dying in their collars and ties and the suits they usually only wear at church, and four MSIV cadets fidget and sweat in their green dress uniforms.

In half an hour they'll be officers. Four years of drudgery, frustration, stress, and fun will end. Eight years of training, garrison, deployment, and combat will begin.

There's Victor Collier, a Morris College grad who branched Military Police. In about two years' time he'll enter the rotation of units serving in Iraq, where military police are in high demand. They escort convoys. They hunt down criminals and insurgents. They guard prisons like Abu Ghraib.

Then there's Willie Martin from Benedict. He branched Armor. He, too, is likely to end up in Iraq, where tanks are the Army's most effective psychological weapon, crawling down ancient city streets, all metal and rubber and noise in a place better suited to compact cars and scrawny beasts of burden. He'll be joined by James Rembert, an Airborne-qualified Benedict grad who also branched Armor.

Last but not least is Jonathan Coe, the slight, young-looking future aviator. Next to Rembert, Martin, and Collier, all three of whom are tall and muscular, Coe looks like a little kid in his daddy's uniform. But he looks cool and confident, too—or at least oblivious. All around him, cadets and their friends and family are sweating and casting surreptitious glances at their watches, but Coe doesn't seem to notice.

A major stands to pray and everyone bows their heads—everyone, that is, except Sergeant Bell, who's been standing in the back with his hands folded over his paunch, making faces at the cadets, and poking at the lone reporter scribbling notes on a legal pad, and who now looks up and around as if trying to locate this "God" person everyone keeps talking to.

The prayer is sedate, Methodist rather than Pentecostal. The major beseeches the Heavenly Father to watch and protect these young men and grant them the wisdom, strength, and compassion to be righteous leaders of men.

Amen.

Heads pop up. Children keep fidgeting. Mothers continue fanning themselves furiously. Bell groans when Moring takes the stand. The colonel gazes lovingly at his officers-to-be and tells them in his characteristically redundant fashion that's he proud of them and all they've done and confident they'll meet the tremendous potential they've demonstrated these past years. And he gestures to the framed commissions he's about to hand out. "You'll keep these and keep them forever," he says, *this close* to weeping with pride and affection.

Before things get too treacly, Moring steps aside and the guest speaker takes his place. A barrel-chested full colonel, the commandant of the Army's recruiting school, Jack Collins looks every inch like the warrior he's not. Sure, he's got plenty of deployments and decorations in his past, but these days he oversees the least dangerous, albeit most suspect, command of the U.S. Army. He trains soldiers to convince civilians that being a soldier is a good idea. With deaths in Iraq nearing one thousand, it's a hell of a hard sell, and by 2004 the Army is having trouble meeting recruitment goals.

There are other signs that the Army's falling apart. With one hundred thousand reservists on active duty, personnel costs are skyrocketing. Wartime wear and tear is sending maintenance costs through the roof. Aviation is losing more choppers than it's buying. Procurement program after procurement program falls prey to the subsequent budget squeeze. And it's not just equipment taking a beating. In August alone, more than a thousand soldiers are wounded in Iraq.

Collins is no fool. He knows exactly the kinds of obstacles the Army faces. Standing before the packed room of cadets, cadre, and sweaty civilians like a low-rent black Patton, Collins declares, "We are a nation at war. This is serious business."

But to Collins, it's not just business. It's a passion.

"I have a love affair with America," Collins says. And so should you is the implication. Collins looks the cadets up and down. "If you don't feel something putting on that uniform, perhaps you're in the wrong business."

There's that word again. Business. On one hand, it's a love affair. On the other, it's a vocation, like selling light fixtures or manufacturing Styrofoam. Collins's rhetoric is just that—rhetoric. But it's enough to make you wonder.

The two hundred thousand Americans in Iraq . . . do they consider the occupation a job, a passion, or both? Do they love pacifying hostile nations? Do they love busting down doors and hog-tying suspected insurgents? Do they love escorting convoy after endless convoy down the dusty roads connecting remote bases? Do they "feel something" when they pull on the same rank, unwashed uniform for the third week in a row?

Maybe they do. Maybe the thousands of soldiers and Marines gathering outside Najaf to take on radical cleric Moqtada al-Sadr's nutball Mahdi Army *do* feel something when they wear the red-white-and-blue patch that tells the world whom they serve: the United States of America. Land of the free. Home of the brave. Et cetera.

Maybe Wil McLean feels something when he's on his twice-daily long-distance run in preparation for Ranger School. In just a few months, he'll be the one killing insurgents on the yellow streets of Iraq. Maybe his gratitude to the Army for being his home will survive contact with an enemy only fighting for *his* home.

Maybe Jennifer Fauth, busy with the day-to-day administrative headache of being battalion commander at USC, finds quiet moments between PT, briefings, labs, and classes to reflect on her future in an Army that considers her a second-class citizen. Maybe her love of the service, and her love of the nation, forgives such minor faults as systematic sexism. Maybe in Iraq she'll find that the Army's restrictions on women in combat are irrelevant. After all, insurgents hate *all* Americans—male, female, whatever. Maybe Fauth'll get ambushed on some Iraqi highway. Maybe she'll get a taste of the combat the Army has tried too hard to keep from her. Maybe it will make all the hassle worthwhile. Maybe she'll feel justified.

And maybe Kim Griggs will fully recover from the shame of flunking Airborne School. Maybe, finally, she'll win the approval of the institution to which she has dedicated her life, the institution she so deeply disappointed when she couldn't make her arms flex, even though she so badly wanted them to. Maybe she'll conquer that one pull-up. Maybe she'll get another shot at Airborne. Maybe she'll get promoted to cadet battalion commander in a couple of years as she's long planned. Maybe she'll get that chance to make the Gamecock Battalion a better place for people like her.

As for John Thorne, maybe the third time's a charm, and his impending deployment to Iraq with the S.C. Guard will go as smoothly as his stints in Bosnia and Cuba did. Maybe he'll survive and return to USC to wrap up his damn business degree so he can finally pin on those lieutenant's bars and start collecting that extra six hundred dollars a month.

As far as Jonathan Coe is concerned, right now there's no maybe. There's no past. There's no future. There's only the bright, shining present, the moment when he stands before God and these witnesses and swears an oath:

I, Jonathan Coe, having been appointed an officer of the United States of America, in the grade of 2nd Lieutenant, do solemnly swear that I will support and defend the Constitution of the United States against all enemies, foreign and domestic, that I will bear true faith and allegiance to the same; that I take this obligation freely, without any mental reservations or purpose of evasion; and that I will well and faithfully discharge the duties of the office upon which I am about to enter; so help me God.

Moring hands him his framed commission, his twin brother pins on his gold bars, and now Coe is an officer in the U.S. Army. He says a few words. He cracks a little joke. But mostly he just smiles, leaving it to Collier to speak for whatever fears may later worm into Coe's heart and the hearts of some four thousand other ROTC cadets facing their futures in an army at war.

Collier stands before the audience, fixes his eyes on the wall, and says in a quavering voice, "I'm not scared at all."